Human Rights
Issues and Challenges

Human Rights
Issues and Challenges

Joseph Benjamin

GYAN

Published by

Gyan Publishing House
5, Ansari Road
Daryaganj, New Delhi-110002
Phone: 011-47034999, 9811692060
E-mail: books@gyanbooks.com

Distribution Network
gyanbooks.com
India, USA, Canada, UK, Australia, France

ISBN: 978-81-212-9080-7

First Published, 2023

Printed at: Gyan Press, Delhi.

HUMAN RIGHTS: ISSUES AND CHALLENGES
Author: JOSEPH BENJAMIN

Contents

Preface

Whenever we think of Human Rights, we are reminded of the UN Declaration of Human Rights of 1948. Human Rights are generally defined as the rights which every human being is supposed to have and are to be protected by the State. All societies, associations even the States have developed certain Rights for their members, people and citizens. People have fought for certain conditions, privileges and Rights in their societies and States. The conception of the rights which every human being is entitled to enjoy only by virtue of being a member of the human species has evolved through history in course of various struggles in the world. Barons in England had to fight for their privileges/rights in 1215 AD and they got them. Magna Carta was issued in June 1215 and can be considered as the first document to put into writing the principle that the king and his government was not above the law. It prevented the king from exploiting his power and put some limitation to King's supremacy in the State. Americans fought for their independence in 1775 and they could threw off British rule from 13 colonies and established United States of America.

Similarly, people of France had to fight for their basic right during French Revolution and finally they got them. All societies had to struggle for certain privileges and they got them. After World War I, League of Nations was established in order to protect the rights of minorities, workers and people. But the idea of human rights emerged stronger after World War II. After the World War II calls came from across the globe for human rights standards to protect citizens from abuses by their governments, standards against which nations could be held accountable for the treatment of those living within their borders. These voices played a very vital role in the

San Francisco meeting that drafted the United Nations Charters in 1945. On December 10, 1948, a document on Rights and freedoms of all human beings was signed by 56 members of the United Nations (The vote was unanimous, although eight nations chose to abstain).

After the signing of Universal Declaration of Human Rights, most of the Nations have inserted certain fundamental Rights/basic rights in their Constitution. Indian Constitution has inserted fundamental Rights in Chapter III and IV of its Constitution. No matter how great a nation be, yet it has to abide and conform to Human Rights Laws. Human Rights Law is superior to all laws of the States. Human Rights are to be abided and protected by all nations. No state can deny Human Rights whatever circumstances may be or arise.

The present book is an attempt to study various issues and challenges of human rights locally and globally. An attempt is made to study, how Human Rights are brazenly violated in India. On various fronts, there is a violation of human rights. Globally, I try to study the various issues like, Foreign Policy, Human Rights and Democracy.

The Chapter on *Indian Constitution and Human Rights: A Symphonise Relationship* is an attempt to study the inter-relation between Indian Constitution and Human Rights. It is found that there is a close connection between Indian Constitution and Human Rights. Various provisions of the Universal Declaration of Human Rights have been inserted in the Chapter III and IV of Indian Constitution. In this chapter an effort is made to study how fundamental rights mentioned in Indian Constitution is similar to human rights mentioned in the Universal Declaration of Human Rights of 1948. An effort will also be made to study how these International Bills have been able to influence the framers of Indian Constitution to include certain provisions of UDHR, 1948.

The Chapter on *Minorities and Human Rights: A Symbiotic Relationship* is an attempt to study the symbiotic relationship between minorities in India and Human Rights Laws. This dwells upon the characteristics of two principles categories of minorities in India, namely religious and linguistic. The minority rights have their due place in the Indian political discourse and are duly protected in the Indian constitutional system.

The Chapter on *B. R. Ambedkar: An Indefatigable Defender of Human Rights* studies how Dr B R Ambedkar fought tirelessly for the rights of untouchables. He is considered to be harbinger of *Dalits* Rights in India.

The Chapter on *Corruption: Violation of Human Rights* is an attempt to study the corruption in India. However, corruption is the violation of Human Rights. This chapter would try to study how corruption is a violation of human rights. This chapter would be confined to corruption in India. Each and every citizen especially women, children have right to development, right to food, right to health etc.

The Chapter on *Violence against Women* is an effort, made to study three critical forms of violence against women, namely, violence in the form of rape, domestic violence, and dowry deaths. This chapter will focus on different types of crimes committed against women in India. Data is based on the NCRB 2021.

The Chapter on *Democracy and Human Rights: A Dialectical Relationship*, focuses on the relationship between democracy and Human Rights. Today most of the countries of twenty-first century have adopted democratic system of government. At the same time there are countries, not practicing democratic pattern of government even though they are the signatories of the UN Declaration of Human Rights of 1948. Are they able to protect the Human Rights of their citizens in their countries? The present study is an attempt to study how non-democratic countries are able to protect Human Right of their citizens. The study will try to find out whether there is any relationship between Democracy and Human Rights at all. The study will find out the true relationships between two concepts, viz., democracy and Human Rights.

The Chapter on *India's Human Rights Diplomacy* discusses with India's foreign policy and Human Rights Laws. The present chapter would focus on India's foreign policy and try to study how India is able to protect and promote Human Rights in India and other part of the world keeping in mind its national interest. An effort is also made to study various factors in formulating foreign policy with other countries States which ensures its national interests.

In preparing this book on **Human Rights: Issues and Challenges**, I have been encouraged by my family members, who have shown their patience during my work.

I will be happy to have comments and feedback on this book entitled, **Human Rights: Issues and Challenges.**

Nagpur: June 15, 2023 **Joseph Benjamin**

List of Tables

1

Indian Constitution and Human Rights: A Symphonise Relationship

The Constituent Assembly met for the first time on December 9, 1946 to draft the Constitution of India. The final draft was submitted to the Constituent Assembly on 25 November 1949. The Constituent Assembly took 2 years 11 months and 18 days to complete drafting the Constitution for free India. The Constitution came into force on 26 January 1950. The drafting committee took the note of national as well as international issues. An effort was made to include the concept of Human Rights in Indian Constitution. The Committee members were very much influenced by the various International Bills concerning to the rights of the people such as Magna Carta of Britain, Bills of Rights of 1688, American Declaration of Impendence of 1766 and the French Declaration of Independence of 1789, etc, Universal Declaration of Human Rights did influence the minds of committee members. It is a unique coincidence that drafting works for the human rights declaration (February, 1947) and the Constitution of India (December, 1946/ October, 1947) began almost simultaneously. The draft Constitution of India was published in February 1948 and finally adopted on 26 November 1949. Under the international influence of and commitment to the human rights, there are more than half of the articles of the Universal Declaration having direct reference in Chapter III of the Indian Constitution enumerating fundamental rights. The Indian State is constitutionally committed to protect and promote the rights of minorities and other deprived peoples, such as women, Other Backward Classes (OBCs), Scheduled Castes (SCs) and Scheduled Tribes (STs). Now the Indian State also provides the benefits to Economically Weaker Sections (EWSs). In this chapter an effort is made to study how fundamental rights mentioned in Indian Constitution is similar to human rights mentioned in the Universal Declaration of Human Rights of 1948. An effort will also be made to study how these International Bills have been able to influence the framers of Indian Constitution.

The Constituent Assembly was influenced by the Sapru Committee Report[1] on Fundamental Rights enshrined in Indian Constitution. It recommended two sets of fundamental rights, namely justiciable and non-justiciable. The Constituent Assembly incorporated these rights of citizens. The Constituent Assembly tried to make India as a welfare state. If one reads each and every word of preamble, one finds that, it contains the basic rights of Indian citizens. The Preamble [2] reads as:

> *"We the people of India, having solemnly resolved to constitute India into a Sovereign Socialist Secular Democratic Republic and to secure to all its citizens:*
>
> *Justice, Social, economic and political;*
>
> *Liberty of thought, expression, belief, faith and worship;*
>
> *Equality of status and of opportunity;*
>
> *and to promote among them all*
>
> *Fraternity assuring the dignity of the individual and the unity and integrity of the nation;*
>
> *In our Constituent Assembly this twenty-sixth day of November, 1949, do hereby adopt, enact and give to ourselves this constitution."*

The Preamble is a part and parcel of the constitution. It is the soul of constitution of India. Chief Justice Sikri once said that, 'Preamble of Indian Constitution is of extreme importance and the constitution should be read and interpreted in the light of the guard and noble vision expressed in the preamble. The preamble is described as a significant instrument which helps us to understand the real intensions of the framers of the constitution. Though there are some fundamental concepts such as socialist and secular were incorporated in the preamble, in late 1970s but it does not mean that our constitution was not secular and socialist in nature.'[3] It was very much prevalent in the Chapter III of Indian Constitution. At the same time, the incorporation of word 'secular' was not new in the preamble. It was there in the Article 25 of Indian Constitution. The amendment was made in the preamble only to give more emphasis.

Again, the term 'democratic' indicates that the constitution has established a form of government which gets its authority from the 'will of the people'. Democracy will be meaningless if it fails to promote brotherhood amongst all sections of the people, a feeling that they are all children of the same soil, the same Motherland. Indian Constitution is against hereditist nature of authority. Liberty, equality, justice and fraternity become the main feature of Indian constitution. Article 1 of the Universal Declaration of Human Rights says: All human being are born free and equal in dignity and rights. They are endowed with reason and conscience and should act towards one another in a spirit of brotherhood. Words, 'democratic' 'republic' assures the people of the right of equal participation in polity. It also means that head of the state would be elected periodically by the people either directly or indirectly.

Fundamental Rights vis-à-vis- Human Rights

Fundamental Rights, considered to be the basic rights of all citizens, are based on the Universal Declaration of Human Rights of 1948. The Chapter III of Indian Constitution is to protect and promote the basic rights of all citizens. It assures that certain liberty and freedoms of people to be respected by the prevailing government. The fundamental rights are guaranteed in Indian Constitution, consisting of Articles 12-35. Article 12 defines the expression of "State". "In this part, unless the context otherwise requires, 'the State' includes the Government and Parliament of India and the Government and the Legislature of each of the State and all local or other authorities within the territories of India or under the control of the Government of India."[4] The Supreme Court of India has expanded the meaning of 'State'. It includes all those bodies which are though not created by the constitution or by the statute, yet are acting as agencies or instrumentalities of the government.[5] Article 13 makes any law inconsistent with or in derogation of the fundamental rights as void to the extent of inconsistency. Article 13 (2) reads: "*The State shall not make any law which takes away or abridges the rights conferred by this Part and any Law made in contravention of this clause shall, to the extent of the contravention, be void.*"

This provision allows judicial review of all legislations made in Indian Parliament and States legislatures. It also prohibits the State to make any law which takes away totally or abrogates any provision of fundamental rights. Any constitutional amendment can be challenged if it violates the 'basic structure' of the constitution.[6]

Almost all rights mentioned in the Chapter III of Indian constitution are the basic rights and cannot be amended or taken away except during the national emergency. Even during the national emergency Article 21 being part of Chapter III cannot be suspended. Most of the provisions of Human Rights mentioned in the Universal Declaration of Human Rights of 1948 can be found in the Chapter III and IV of Indian Constitution. They constitute the basic structure of constitution as they are essential for development of personality for each and every individual. That's why they cannot be abrogated by a constitutional amendment.[7]

Six basic rights to its citizens have been mentioned in Article 14 to 35 in Indian constitution.[8] These rights are: right to equality, (article 14-18), right to freedom (19-22), right against exploitation (23-24), right to freedom of religion (25-28), cultural and educational rights (29-30), and right to constitutional remedies (32-35). In this chapter, an attempt is made to study all fundamental rights mentioned in Indian Constitution and try to find out how these rights are similar/ close to the provisions of Universal Declaration of Human Rights and other International bodies.

Right to Equality

The right to equality is the soul and creed of Indian democratic republic. It forms the foundation of socio-economic justice. Article 14 embodies the idea of equality as expressed in the preamble. Article 14 provides: the State shall not deny to any person equality before the law or legal protection of the laws within the territory of India. Article 14 of Indian constitution is similar to Articles 1 and 7 of the Universal Declaration of Human Rights of 1948. Article 7 of the Universal Declaration of Human Rights says: *All are equal before law and are entitled without any discrimination to equal protection of law. All are entitled to equal protection against any discrimination in violation of this declaration and against any incitement to such discrimination.*[9] At the same time Article 14 of Indian Constitution is seen very close to Articles 2 (2) and 3 of the International Covenant on Economic, Social and Cultural Rights, 1966 and the International Covenant on Civil and Political Rights. The reference to the principles of equality and non-discrimination is also found in the Charter of United Nation which says: *All human beings are born free and equal in dignity and rights. They are endowed with reason and conscience and should act towards one another in a spirit of brotherhood.*[10] Other International bodies also prescribe the same principles that is 'the elimination of all forms of racial discrimination among all human beings.[11] Similarly, the Article 14 of Indian Constitution talks about equality before law and equal protection of the laws. Applying the general principle of Article 15 of the Indian Constitution specifically prohibits discrimination on the grounds of religion, race, caste, sex or place of birth. Article 15 speaks:-

1. *The State Shall not discriminate against any citizen on ground only of religion, race, caste, sex, place of birth or any of them.*
2. *No citizen shall, on grounds only of religion, race, caste, sex, place of birth or any of them, be subject to any disability, liability, restriction or condition with regard to-*
   (a) *Access to shops, public restaurant, hotel and place of public entertainment; or*
   (b) *The use of wells, tanks, bathing ghats, roads and places of public resort maintained wholly or partly out of State funds or dedicated to the use of the general public.*
3. *Nothing in this article shall prevent the State from making any special provision for women and children.*

Article 15 (4) and (5) permits the State to make special provision for the advancement of disadvantaged groups such as Scheduled Castes (SCs) and Scheduled Tribes (STs), and Other Backward Classes (OBCs). The Scheduled Castes and Scheduled Tribes are provided reservation in three fields, namely education, employment and political. Similarly Other Backward Classes are given reservation in the field of education and employment. The leaders have justified that since they (SCs, STs and OBCs) were not equal for centuries, the reservation provisions have been made to make them equal. But today it is considered as vote bank for certain political parties. There had an attempt in past to reserve 33 percent seats in the parliament for women. But this has not been passed yet.

Article 16 of Indian Constitution aims at providing equality of opportunity to all citizens in the matters of public employment. Article 16 speaks:-

1. *There shall be equality of opportunity for all citizens in matters relating to employment or appointment to any office under the State.*
2. *No citizen shall, on grounds only religion, race, caste, sex, descent, place of birth, residence or any of them, be ineligible for, or discriminated against in respect of, any employment or office under the State.*
3. *Nothing in this article shall prevent Parliament from making any law prescribing, in regard to a class or classes of employment or appointment to an office (under the Government of, or any local or other authority within, a State or Union Territory, any requirement as to residence within that State or Union Territory) prior to such employment or appointment.*

Article 21 (2) of the Universal Declaration of Human Rights 1948 says that "*everyone has the right to equal access to public services in his country.*" Indian leaders have been using reservation as a potent weapon for assuring their votes and do not fill the sanctioned post.

Table 1: ***Teaching post vacant in central universities in India***

Category	Assistant Professors	Associate Professors	Pro-fessors	Category and Percentage of share of total vacancies
Open Category	12.9%	25.08%	45.07%	21.1%
SC Vacancies	20.3%	64.6%	75.2%	39.7%
ST Vacancies	26.9%	76.8%	87.3%	71.8
OBCs Vacancies	28.8%	76.5%	84.7%	45.1%

Source: Data Shared by Ministry of Education in Lok Sabha on December 12, 2022.

The Mandal Commission agitation in the year 1990 is a clear example of this. After 1990 agitation of OBCs, the Government of India has agreed to reserve seats for OBCs in higher educational institutes in 2008.

Article 17 of Indian Constitution abolishes untouchability and its practice in any form would be punishable. This article reads, *Untouchability is abolished and its practice in any form is forbidden. The enforcement of any disability arising out of 'Untouchability' shall be an offence punishable in accordance with law.* The present article of Indian Constitution is close to the Article 2 of the Universal Declaration of Human Rights. Protest against untouchability is very similar to the protest against racial discrimination in South Africa and Namibia. Now racial discrimination in South Africa has been abolished and they have their own government.

Indian Government has enacted various Acts in order to prohibit untouchability in any form in Indian society. After Independence, parliament passed an Act which is known as Untouchability (Offences) Act 1955. This Act bans untouchability in any form in Indian society. Again in 1976, this Act was amended in order to make the law more stringent for removing untouchability from our society. This Act has now been renamed as 'the Protection of Civil Rights Act 1955'. Under the amended Act any discrimination on the ground of untouchability, it is considered as an offence. The public servants have been asked to investigate the matter. The Supreme Court of India has held that the fundamental right under Article 17 of Indian Constitution is available against private individual also and it is the constitutional duty of the State to take action against violators and ensure that fundamental right is not violated in any circumstances in Indian society.[12]

Right to Freedom

Articles 19 to 22 deals with varieties of freedoms to each and every citizen in India. Freedom is viewed as the most precious human value which is very much present in Article 19 of Indian Constitution. Indian Constitution provides six basic fundamental freedoms to all its citizens. It provides to all citizens:-

(a) To freedom of speech and expression;

(b) To assembly peacefully and without arms;

(c) To form associations or unions;

(d) To move freely throughout the territories of India;

(e) To reside and settle in any part of the territories of India;

(g) To practice any profession, or to carry on any occupation, trade or business.

Democracy without freedom of speech and expression is not possible. It is very similar to Article 19 of the International Covenant on Civil and Political Rights of 1966. Article 19 (1) (b) of Indian Constitution guarantees all citizens freedom of peaceful assembly without arms. This provision of Indian Constitution is also similar to Article 20 (1) of the Universal Declaration of Human Rights 1948 which also says: Everyone has the right to freedom of peaceful assembly and association. The right to peaceful assembly is also recognised in Article 21 of the International Covenant on Civil and Political Rights, 1966. This right is available in almost all democratic countries of the world.

Article 19 (1) (c) of the Indian Constitution guarantees to all its citizens the right to form associations or unions. This right is very similar to Article 23 (4) of the Universal Declaration of Human Rights, 1948. This provision is also prevalent in Article 22 of the International Covenant on Civil and Political Rights, 1966 and article 8 of the International Covenant on Economic, Social and Cultural Rights, 1966 and also very close to Article 13 of the Universal Declaration of Human Rights, 1948.

Similarly, Indian Constitution provides its citizens the right to move freely throughout the territory of India or to reside and settle in any part of the country but this right shall be subject to restrictions imposed by the State in the interest of the general public or for the protection of any Scheduled Tribe. One can see this in Northeast States. Entry in these States is restricted.

Article 20 of Indian Constitution provides Protection in respect of conviction for offences. It says:-

(1) *No person shall be convicted of any offence except for violation of a law in force at the time of the commission of*

the Act charged as an offence, nor be subjected to a penalty greater than that which might have been inflicted under the law in force at the time of the commission of the offence.

(2) *No person shall be prosecuted and punished for the same offence more than once.*

(3) *No person accused of any offence shall be compelled to be a witness against himself.*

The Article 11(2) of the Universal Declaration of Human Rights is similar to the Article 20 of Indian Constitution. Article 11 (2) of the Universal Declaration of Human Rights says: "No one shall be held guilty of any penal offence on account of any act or omission which did not constitute a penal offence, under national or international law, at the time when it was committed. Nor shall a heavier penalty be imposed than the one that was applicable at the time the penal offence was committed." A provision similar to Article 20 (1) is also found in Article 15 (1) of the International Covenant on Civil and Political Rights. Article 20 (1) of Indian Constitution provides protection against *ex post facto* law and thus prohibits the legislature to make retrospective criminal law. This clause protects the basic human right of the people that no person can be punished for an act which was not an offence at the date of its commission. It also protects the person by providing that no person could be subjected to a penalty greater than that which might have inflicted under the law in force at the time of the commission of the offence.

Protection of Life and Personal Liberty

No person shall be deprived of his/her life or personal liberty except according to procedure established by law. Right to life and personal liberty is most fundamental of all fundamental rights. This article is most important among all basic rights of individuals. During the time of national emergency, all rights of citizens will be suspended but this right to life and personal liberty cannot be suspended in any circumstances. Article 21 says:-

"No person shall be deprived of his life or personal liberty except according to procedure established by law."

This article of Indian Constitution highlights the objective of Article 3 of the Universal Declaration of Human Rights which says; "Everyone has the right to life, liberty and security of person." This provision is also prevalent in Article 6 of the International Covenant on Civil and Political Rights. This right is given to citizens as well as non-citizens. The term 'personal liberty' has been made clear by the former Justice P N Bhagwati in a famous case, Maneka Gandhi *v* Union of India in 1978.[13] He observed that, *"the expression 'personal liberty' in article 21 is of the widest amplitude and it covers a variety of rights which go to constitute the personal liberty of men and some of them have been raised to the status of distinct fundamental rights and given additional protection under Article 19.*" He was further of the opinion that the attempt of the Court should be to expand the reach and ambit of the fundamental rights rather than attenuate their meaning and content by a process of judicial construction.[14] Justice Krishna Iyer in the same case took the view that even the law under Article 21 must also be "just, fair and reasonable."[15]

This new interpretation of Article 21 of Indian constitution which explains its nature, scope and ambit has resulted in the development of a new Human Rights constitutional jurisprudence. No doubt all rights given in fundamental rights are enforceable in the court of law. There were numbers of cases which helped judges to see Article 21 from different angles and different perspectives. The meaning of Article 21 can be seen as a right to live in healthy environment and right to maintenance and improvement of public health. Various interpretation of Article 21 of Indian Constitution will certainly help in achieving the objectives of corresponding Article 26 of the Universal Declaration of Human Rights. Thus, Article 21 can be interpreted as the heart of human rights. Right to education has now been added as fundamental rights in Indian constitution. Thus, Article 21 A, Right to Education, says, "The State shall provide free and compulsory education to all children of the age of six to fourteen years in such manner as the State may, by law, determine."[16] One can also find the right to education recognised in Article 13 (2 a) of the International Covenant on Economic, Social and Cultural Rights. It says, "Primary education shall be compulsory and available free to all."

Article 22 of the Constitution deals with protections against arrest and detention in certain cases. Article 22 says,

(1) *No person who is arrested shall be detained in custody without being informed, as soon as may be, of the grounds for such arrest nor shall be denied the right to consult, and to be defended by, a legal practitioner of his choice.*

(2) *Every person who is arrested and detained in custody shall be produced before the nearest magistrate within a period of twenty-four hours of such arrest excluding the time necessary for the journey from the place of arrest to the court of magistrate and no such person shall be detained in custody beyond the said period without the authority of a magistrate.*

(3) *Nothing in clause (1) and (2) shall apply-*

  (a) *To any person who for the time being is an enemy alien, or*

  (b) *To any person who is arrested or detained under any law providing for preventive detention.*

(4) *No law providing for preventive detention shall authorise the detention of a person for a longer period than three months unless-*

  (a) *An Advisory Board consisting of persons who are, or have been, or are qualified to be appointed as, Judges of a High Court has reported before the expiration of the said period of three months that there is in its opinion sufficient cause for such detention:*

  Provided that nothing in this sub-clause shall authorise the detention of any person beyond the maximum period prescribed by any law made by Parliament under sub-clause (b) of clause (7); or

  (b) *Such person is detained in accordance with the provisions of any law made by Parliament under sub-clause (a) and (b) of clause (7).*

(5) *When any person is detained in pursuance of an order made under any law providing for preventive detention, the authority making the order shall, as soon as may be,*

communicate to such person the grounds on which the order has been made and shall afford him the earliest opportunity of making a representation against the order.

(6) *Nothing in clause (5) shall require the authority making any such order as is referred to in that clause to disclose facts which such authority considers to be against the public interest to disclose.*

(7) *Parliament may by law prescribe-*

(a) *The circumstances under which, and the class or classes of cases in which, a person may be detained for a period longer than three months under any law providing for preventive detention without obtaining the opinion of an Advisory Board in accordance with the provisions of sub-clause (a) of clause (4);*

(b) *The maximum period for which any person may in any class or classes of cases be detained under any law providing for preventive detention; and*

(c) *The procedure to be followed by an Advisory Board in an inquiry under sub-clause (a) of clause (4).*

The people of India have experienced the gravest abuse of the preventive detention power during the 1975 Emergency when a large number of persons were preventively detained under Maintenance of Internal Security Act 1971 (MISA), in utter disregard of the law. Even the judicial attitude was not fully in favour of the detainees.[17] Certain changes have been made in MISA in 1978 according 44th Constitutional Amendment Act.

Similar law known as Unlawful Activities Prevention Act of 2019 is being practiced frequently. In India, we have been using UAPA (Unlawful Activities Prevention Act) and many have been detained in jail for years. The main objective of this law was to make powers available for dealing with activities directed against the integrity and sovereignty of India. The most recent amendment of the law, the Unlawful Activities (Prevention) Amendment act, 2019 (UAPA 2019) has made it possible for the Centre Government to designate individuals as terrorists without a due process of law. No doubt this Act is against the Human Rights as immediate bail is not granted in this case. United Nations' special rapporteurs stated that the provision of the UAPA 2019 contravenes several articles of the Universal Declaration of Human Rights and the International Covenant on Civil and Political Rights as Article 9 of the Universal Declaration of Human Rights says; "No one shall be subjected to arbitrary arrest, detention or exile."[18] Generally bail was not granted in UAPA, but the Supreme has granted bail in the Watali case (2002). (N/A vs. Zohoor Ahmad Shah Watali)

Now the Supreme Court has asked the Centre the validity of Sedition Action. On May 11, 2022, the Supreme Court has directed that all pending trials, appeals, and proceedings on the charges under the Indian Penal Code's (IPC) Section 124A, which deals with sedition, be kept in abeyance until the Central Government completes a re-examination of the provision. What is Sedition Law as per Section 124A? Sedition Law according to Section 124A defines sedition as, "Whoever, by words, either spoken or written, or by signs or by visible representation or otherwise, brings or attempts to bring into hatred or contempt or excites or attempts to excite disaffection towards, the Government established by law shall be punished with imprisonment for life, to which fine may be added." Many have filed a petition against this section. Journalists, Member of Parliament and others have argued that this section is against the human rights. Many countries have repealed this in their respective countries. This section is against the Universal Declaration of Human Rights and also against the International Covenant on Civil and Political Rights. Article 9 (1) of the International Covenant on Civil and Political Rights 1966 says; "Everyone has the right to liberty and security of person. No one shall be subjected to arbitrary arrest or detention. No one shall be deprived of his liberty except on such grounds and in accordance with such procedure as are established by law."

Freedom against Exploitation

Article 23 of Indian Constitution prohibits the traffic in human beings and begar and other similar forms of forced labour. The Constitutional provision says:

(1) *Traffic in human beings and begar and other similar forms of forced labour are prohibited and any contravention of*

this provision shall be an offence punishable in accordance with law.

(2) *Nothing in this article shall prevent the State from imposing compulsory service for public purposes, and in imposing such service the State shall not make any discrimination on grounds only of religion, race, caste, or class or any of them.*

Compelling any human being for begging on the street is prohibited as per the Indian Constitution. At the same time no human being can be forced to be transported to anywhere for forced labour. Women cannot be forced to brothel anywhere. The provision of Indian Constitution corresponds to Article 4 of the Universal Declaration of Human Rights and also to Article 8 of the International Covenant on Economic, Social and Cultural Rights. Article 4 of the Universal Declaration of Human Rights says; "No one shall be held in slavery or servitude; slavery and the slave trade shall be prohibited in all forms." "Traffic in human beings" is meant for buying and selling human beings for different purposes, illegal work, forced labour and sexual purposes. Traffic in human beings is prohibited. This article also prohibits force labour. We, even today, find many forced labours in India. Effort has been taken to liberate the bonded labour or forced labour in India. The Parliament has enacted the Bonded Labour System (Abolition) Act, 1976 to solve the problem of Bonded Labour in India.

The Article of 24 of the Indian Constitution prohibits employment of children in factories and especially hazardous factories. Article says, "*No child below the age of fourteen years shall be employed to work in any factory or mine or engaged in any other hazardous employment.*" This article protects the rights of Children and they should not be exploited. Their tender age should not be exploited by any landlords in agrarian field in rural areas or big industrialists in cities. Their age is to be in the school and not in any industry. They should be encouraged to attend schools. That's why the government of India has come out with another article in the constitution that is Article 21A. It says, "*The State shall provide free and compulsory education to all children of the age of six to fourteen years in such manner as the State may, by law, determine.*" With the help of Central government, States have started mid-day meal in many schools so that children need not go to the field to work and this way Gross Enrolment Ratio has been increased. The main goal of National Education Policy 2020 has the same intension. Likewise, Article 32 (1) of the Convention on the Rights of the Child 1989 says; "State Parties recognize the right of the child to be protected from economic exploitation and from performing any work that is likely to be hazardous or to interfere with the child's education, or to be harmful to the child's health or physical, mental, spiritual, moral or social development."

Right to Freedom of Religion

India is a secular State. It means it is neither religious, nor anti-religious. It will not promote any religion and hence, it only follows constitution. Right to freedom of religion has four articles, 25, 26, 27 and 28. Article 25 provides freedom of conscience and free profession, practice and propagation of religion:-

(1) *Subject to public order, morality and health and to the other provisions of this Part, all persons are equally entitled to freedom of conscience and the right freely to profess, practise and propagate religion.*[19]

(2) *Nothing in this article shall affect the operation of any existing law or prevent the State from making any law-*

   (a) *regulating or restricting any economic, financial, political or other secular activity which may be associated with religious practice;*

   (b) *providing for social welfare and reform or the throwing open of Hindu religious institutions of a public character to all classes and sections of Hindus.*

Again Article 26 provides freedom to manage religious affairs of any religion. It says, subject to public order, morality and health, every religious denominations or an section thereof shall have the following rights-

(a) *to establish and maintain institutions for religious and charitable purposes;*

(b) *to manage its own affairs in matters of religion;*

(c) *to own and acquire movable and immovable property; and*

(d) *To administer such property in accordance with law.*

The Constitution of India does not allow payment of Tax for the promotion of particular religion. Article 27 says, "No person shall be compelled to pay any taxes, the proceeds of which are specifically appropriated in payment of expenses for the promotion or maintenance of any particular religion or religious denomination." Again Article 28 of Indian Constitution does not allow anyone to provide religious instruction in an educational institution. Article 28 says,

(1) *No religious instruction shall be provided in any educational institution wholly maintained out of State funds.*

(2) *Nothing in clause (1) shall apply to an educational institution which is administered by the State but has been established under any endowment or trust which requires that religious instruction shall be imparted in such institution.*

(3) *No person attending any educational institution recognised by the State or receiving aid out of State funds shall be required to take part in any religious instruction that may be imparted in such institution or to attend any religious worship that may be conducted in such institution or in any premises attached thereto unless such person or, if such person is a minor, his guardian has given his consent thereto.*

India is a multi-religious country, where there is no State religion as one can see in other countries. It means India is a secular country where all religions are given equal respect. The word secular means that, India will be neither religious, nor anti-religious, nor irreligious.[20] Article 28 clearly states that schools/colleges cannot give any religious instruction fully funded by the State. The secular nature of Indian society demands mutual tolerance of different religious faith and belief. This article provides each and every citizen to promote, practice and propagate ones religious affairs. This article is very close to Universal Declaration of Human Rights, the right to equality.

Articles 29 and 30 of Indian Constitution provide cultural and educational rights of minorities in India. Article 29 says,

(1) *Any section of the citizens residing in the territory of India or any part thereof having a distinct language, script or culture of its own shall have the right to conserve the same.*

(2) *No citizen shall be denied admission into any educational institution maintained by the State or receiving aid out of State funds on grounds only of religion, race, caste, language or any of them.*

Article 30 of Indian Constitution allows minorities, whether minorities based on language or religion to establish educational institutions and manage, administer those institutions. Minority institutions have been given certain rights to provide reservation for their own communities that may be based on language or religion. Article 30 says,

(1) *All minorities, whether based on religion or language, shall have the right to establish and administer educational institutions of their choice.*

(1A) *In making any law providing for the compulsory acquisition of any property of an educational institution established and administered by a minority, referred to in clause (1), the State shall ensure that the amount fixed by or determined under such law for the acquisition of such property is such as would not restrict or abrogate the right guaranteed under that clause.*[21]

(2) *The State shall not, in granting aid to educational institutions, discriminate against any educational institution on the ground that it is under the management of a minority, whether based on religion or language.*

This provision of Indian Constitution is very close to Article 18 of the Universal Declaration of Human Rights which says; "Everyone has the right to freedom of thought, conscience and religion; this includes freedom to change his religion or belief, and freedom, either alone or in community with others and in public or private, to manifest his religion or belief in teaching, practice, worship and observance." This provision of Indian Constitution is also close to Article 27 of the International Covenant on Civil and Political Rights. It says: "In those State in which ethnic, religious or linguistic minorities exist, persons belonging to such minorities shall not be denied the right, in community with the other members of their group, to enjoy their own culture, to profess and practise their own religion, or to use their own language."

Right to Constitutional Remedies

Article 32 provides right to Constitutional remedies to its citizens. Article 32 says,

(1) *The right to move the Supreme Court by appropriate proceedings for the enforcement of the rights conferred by this Part is guaranteed.*

(2) *The Supreme Court shall have power to issue directions or orders or writs, including writs in the nature of habeas corpus, mandamus, prohibition, quo warranto, and certiorari, whichever may be appropriate for the enforcement of any of the rights conferred by this part.*

(3) *Without prejudice to the powers conferred on the Supreme Court by clause (1) and (2), Parliament may by law empower any other court to exercise within the local limits of its jurisdiction all or any of the powers exercisable by the Supreme Court under Clause (2).*

(4) *The rights guaranteed by this Article shall not be suspended except as otherwise provided for by this Constitution.*

All human rights have been considered as fundamental rights and these rights have to be enforced by the apex judicial body. If rights of citizens are being infringed by either by the State governments or Central government, citizens have given rights to approach court for the enforcement their rights. In any circumstance, fundamental rights of Indian citizens cannot be taken away by any government. It is true, fundamental rights can be suspended during emergency. All rights can be suspended, except right to life and personal liberty. Courts have been given right to issue certain writs for the enforcement of rights. The Indian Parliament has the rights to make law on Human Rights of citizens which are enshrined in Indian Constitution as fundamental rights (article 12-35), Directive Principles of State Policies or any other constitutional rights, but the basis structure of Constitution should not be changed.

If law made by the Parliament and if it is not in consonant with the Constitution, citizens have a rights to challenge those law in the court of law. If the law made by the parliament, are not consonant with the constitution, the court has a rights to declare that law as un-constitution or ultra-virus. Article 226 of Indian Constitution confers powers on all the High Courts to issue the writs, orders or directions for the enforcement of six fundamental rights. The article 32 (1) guarantees the fundamental right to its citizens to move to Supreme Court by an appropriate proceeding for the enforcement of rights mentioned in Chapter III of Indian Constitution. Again Article 32(2) empowers the Supreme Court to issue writs, orders or directions for the enforcement of fundamental rights. These provisions of Indian Constitution (article 32), is similar to the 8th article of the Universal Declaration of Human Rights which clearly says: Everyone has the right to an effective remedy by the competent national tribunals for acts violating the fundamental rights granted him by the constitution or by law. This provision of Indian Constitution is very close to Article 2 (3) (a) of the International Covenant on Civil and Political Rights.

Directive Principles of State Policies and Human Rights

Directive Principal of State Policies as given in part IV of Indian Constitution (Article 36-51) is very close to the Universal Declaration of Human Rights. Directive Principles of State Policies aim at the welfare of its citizens in Indian society. The drafters of Indian Constitution understood that by merely incorporating certain rights for citizens will not be enough for their development. Hence, they inserted certain provisions (Article 36-51) in Indian Constitution for development of society as well as the citizens. Article 36 of Part IV provides that in Part III, the meaning of 'State' shall have the same as given in Article 12. The provision in this part shall not be forced by court to apply those schemes for development of society as well as for citizens. Provision mentioned in Part III can be enforced by court.

Article 37 says, "The provision contained in this Part shall not be enforceable by any court, but the principles therein laid down are nevertheless fundamental in the governance of the country and it shall be the duty of the State to apply these principles in making laws."

Article 37 makes it very clear that Part IV of Indian Constitution is not enforceable by any Court. All these provision mentioned in this Part, are only a directions for the State. It is the duty of State to respect these provisions of State. Directive Principles of State Policies provides socio-economic rights of citizens.

Article 38 provides State to secure a social order for the promotion of welfare of the people. It further says,

(1) *The State shall strive to promote the welfare of the people by securing and protecting as effectively as it may a social order in which justice, social, economic and political, shall inform all the institutions of the national life.*

(2) *The State shall, in particular, strive to minimize the inequalities in income and endeavour to eliminate inequalities in status, facilities and opportunities, not only amongst individuals but also amongst groups of people residing in different areas or engaged in different vocations.*

It is the duty of State to promote social welfare of the people by securing socio-economic justice to each citizen of country. One can see that Article 38 of Indian Constitution reflects the spirit of Articles 28 and 29 of the Universal Declaration of Human Rights. Article 28 of the Universal Declaration of Human Rights reads: Everyone is entitled to a social and international order in which the rights and freedoms set forth in this Declaration. Again, the Article 38 (2) of Indian Constitution focuses on equality among all groups of people. This provision was not there in the original constitution and this provision was added in the Constitution by the 44th Amendment Act, 1978 and now this provision is similar to Articles 2 (3) and 3 of the International Covenant on Economic, Social and Cultural Rights which says: "Developing countries, with due regard to human rights and their national economy, may determine to what extend they would guarantee the economic rights recognised in the present Covenant to non-nationals." Similarly Article 3 also reads; "The States Parties to the present Covenant undertake to ensure the equal right of men and women to the enjoyment of all economic, social and cultural rights set forth in the present Covenant."

Directive Principles of State policies generally focus on the welfare of people and hence, Article 39 of Part IV of Indian

Constitution speaks of welfare of Indian Citizens. Article 39 says, that the State shall in particular direct its policy towards securing:-

(a) *That the citizens, men and women equally, have the right to an adequate means of livelihood;*

(b) *That the ownership and control of the material resources of the community are so distributed as best to sub-serve the common good;*

(c) *That the operation of the economic system does not result in the concentration of wealth and means of production to the common detriment;*

(d) *That there is equal pay for equal work for both men and women;*

(c) *That the health and strength of workers, men and women and the tender age of children are not abused and that citizens are not abused and that citizens are not forced by economic necessity to enter avocations unsuited to their age or strength;*

(f) *That children are given opportunities and facilities to develop in a healthy manner and in conditions of freedom and dignity and that childhood and youth are protected against exploitation and against moral and material abandonment.*

The Constitution of India directs the State to formulate policies for the welfare of its citizens. Article 39 (a) put some obligations on the State to provide its citizens the adequate livelihood. The State may take number of measures for certain communities, like women, children for their development. The State may take affirmative action for certain section of society. Clause (b) and (c) of Article 39 can be described as "the charter of economic democracy" and "the charter of the poor man."[22] These two clause of Article 39 promotes the objective of establishing a social welfare State where there will not be concentration of wealth in the hand of few people. It talks of equal distribution of wealth. On the basis of this clauses there was land reform in India and lands were taken from rich people and distributed to landless workers. The Land Reform and equitable distribution of wealth is similar to Article 11 clause 2(a) and (b) of the International Covenant on Economic, Social and Cultural Rights, 1966.

Article 39 (d) speaks of equal pay for equal work irrespective sex. This provision is similar to Article 23(2) of the Universal Declaration of Human Rights and Article 7(a) (i) of the International Covenant on Economic, Social and Cultural Rights, 1966.

The main goal of Article 39 (e) is to provide good health of workers, especially women and children. It also warns State to check that children do not take any hazardous job. Article 39 (f) expects the State to direct its policies in such a manner so as to provide opportunities and facilities to children to develop in a healthy manner and in conditions of freedom and dignity, which are supposed to be children's fundamental rights. It should be a learning procedural. New article has been inserted in 1976, and this is called Article 39-A. It was inserted according to 42nd Amendment Act 1976. It says,

"The State shall secure that the operation of the legal system promotes justice, on a basis of equal opportunity, and shall, in particular provide free legal aid, by suitable legislation or schemes or in any other way, to ensure that opportunities for securing justice are not denied to any citizens by reason of any economic or other disabilities."

This article says that to seek justice is a very important for human right. Ultimately justice must be given. Article 38-A provides constitutional status of free legal aid to the poor and try to remove inequality in access to justice being abolished. The Parliament has also enacted "Legal Services Authority Act, 1987" to achieve objectives of Article 39-A of the Constitution. Articles 41 to 43 provides number of rights to Indian citizens.

Article 41 says, *The State shall, within the limits of its economic capacity and development, make effective provision for securing the right to work, to education and to public assistance in cases of unemployment, old age, sickness and disablement, and in other cases of undeserved want.*

Article 42 says, *"The State shall make provision for securing just and humane conditions of work and for maternity relief."* Hence State provides maternity leave with full pay three to six months. At the same time, States create a conducive atmosphere in the work place and provide leisure time for workers. It is the fundamental rights of workers to have leisure period between their work timing. This provision is similar to Article 25 (1 and 2) of the Universal Declaration of Human Rights, which reads, Motherhood and Childhood are entitled to special care and assistance. All children, whether born in or out of wedlock, shall enjoy the same social protection.

Article 43 says, *"The State shall endeavor to secure, by suitable legislation or economic organisation or in any other way, to all workers, agricultural, industrial or otherwise, work, a living wage, conditions of work ensuring a decent standard of life and full enjoyment of leisure and social and cultural opportunities and, in particular, the State shall endeavour to promote cottage industries on an individual or co-operative basis in rural areas."* This was a dream of Mahatma Gandhi to establish cottage industries in rural areas. The State from time to time revises the daily wages for workers. These Articles 41 to 43 are similar to Articles 23 (1, 2 and 3), 24 and 25 of the Universal Declaration of Human Rights and Articles 6, 7 and 10 (2) of the International Covenant on Economic, Social and Cultural Rights.

Article 43-A has been inserted in Indian Constitution according to 42nd Amendment Act 1976. This article allows the workers participation in the functioning of factories, industries. Today, workers have a right to participate in the functioning of management of industries.

Article 45 says, *"The State shall endeavour to provide early childhood case and education for all children until they complete the age of six years."*[23] This provision is similar to Article 26 of the Universal Declaration of Human Rights which says: *"Everyone has a right to education. Education shall be free, at least in the elementary and fundamental stages. Elementary education shall be compulsory...."* This provision is also similar to Articles 13 and 14 of the International Covenant on Economic, Social and Cultural Rights. The State should raise the level of nutrition and standard of living and improve public health system. Delhi has started primary health centers, *muhala* clinics in different parts of Delhi for all. As Article 47 says, *"The State shall regard the raising of the level of nutrition and the standard of living of its people and the improvement of public health as among its primary duties and, in particular, the State shall endeavour to bring about prohibition of the consumption, except for medicinal purposes of intoxicating drinks and of drugs which are injurious to health."* This very provision is very similar to article 25(1) of the Universal Declaration of Human Rights and Articles 11(1) & (2) and 12 (1) of the International Covenant on Economic, Social and Cultural Rights.

In 1976, a new Article 48-A was added in Chapter IV of Indian Constitution (42nd Amendment Act, 1976) which says, "*The State shall endeavor to protect and improve the environment and to safeguard the forest and wild life of the country.*"

In this regard article 12(2) (b) of the International Covenant on Economic, Social and Cultural Rights is relevant which says, "The Steps to be taken by the States Parties to the present Covenant to achieve the full realisation of this right shall include those necessary for the improvement of all aspects of environmental and industrial hygiene."

The last article of the Directive Principles of State Policies, i.e. Articles 51 speaks of promotion of international peace and security. It says, that the State shall endeavour to,

(a) Promote international peace and security,
(b) Maintain just and honourable relations between nations,
(c) Foster respect for international law and treaty obligations in the dealings of organised people with one another, and
(d) Encourage settlement of international disputes by arbitration.

These provisions mention in Article 51 compels State to maintain just and honourable relations with other nations and foster respect for international law and treaty obligations in dealing with the people. All these provisions given in chapter IV of Indian Constitution correspond to various provisions of the Universal Declaration of Human Rights and other International Covenant on Economic, Social and Cultural Rights, International Covenant on Civil and Political Rights. It has become an obligation of the State to respect the international instruments on Human Rights and achieve their underline goals by applying these constitutional provisions.

Fundamental Duties

Rights and Duties go side by side. If rights are given to citizens, certain duties must be assigned to citizens. Both can be considered as two facet of the same coin. Chapter III provides certain rights to its citizens, whereas Part IV A, Article 51A provides certain duties. Article 51 A was not there in the original text of the Constitution. It was added in Indian Constitution in 1976 by the 42nd amendment Act of Constitution. It has specified ten duties to its citizens. They are:

(a) To abide by the Constitution and respect its ideals and institutions, the National Flag and the National Anthem;

(b) To cherish and follow the noble ideals which inspired our national struggle for freedom;

(c) To uphold and protect the sovereignty, unity and integrity of India;

(d) To defend the country and render national service when called upon to do so;

(e) To promote harmony and the spirit of common brotherhood amongst all people of India transcending religious, linguistic and regional or sectional diversities; to renounce practices derogatory to the dignity of women;

(f) To value and preserve the rich heritage of our composite culture;

(g) To protect and improve the natural environment including forests, lakes, rivers, wild life and to have compassion for living creatures;

(h) To develop the scientific temper, humanism and the spirit of inquiry and reform;

(i) To safeguard public property and adjure violence;

(j) To strive towards excellence in all spheres of individual and collective activity so that the nation constantly rises to higher levels of endeavour and achievement.

(k) Who is a parent or guardian, to provide opportunities for education to his child or, as the case may be, ward between the age of six and fourteen years. (this was added by the constitution 86th Amendment Act 2002, 12-12-2002).

Table 2: ***Table shows the compatibility of Human Rights enshrined in the Universal Declaration of Human Rights (Civil and Political Rights),*** **(Economic, Social and Cultural)** ***and the Indian Constitution.***

Civil and Political Rights

Sl. No.	Universal Declaration of Human Rights	Indian Constitution
1.	Everyone has the right to life, liberty and security of persons (Art 3)	Article 21
2.	No one shall be held in slavery or servitude: slavery and the slave trade shall be prohibited in all their forms (Article 4)	Article 23
3.	Equality before law and non-discrimination (Article 7)	Article 14 & 15
4.	Right to Effective Remedy (Article 8)	Article 32
5.	Rights Against Arbitrary arrest, detention and Right to Habeas Corpus (Article 9)	Article 22
6.	Rights ex-post facto law (Article 11 (2))	Article 20 (1)
7.	Right to freedom of movement (Article 13 (1)	Article (1) d
8.	Right to freedom of thought, Conscience and Religion (Article 18)	Article 25 (1)
9.	Right to Freedom of Opinion and Expression (Article 19)	Article 19(1)a
10.	Right to Freedom of Peaceful Assembly and Association (Article 20 (1)	Article 19 (1) b
11.	Right to Equal Access to Public Service (Article 21 (1)	Article 16 (1)
12.	Right to Social Security (Article 22)	Article 29 (1)
13.	Right to Form and Join Trade Unions (Article 23)	Article 19 (1) c

Economic, Social and Cultural

Sl. No.	Universal Declaration of Human Rights	Indian Constitution
1.	Right to Work. To free choice of an Employment, To just and favourable conditions of work etc., (Article 23 (1)	Article 41
2.	Right to equal pay for Equal Work, Condition of Work etc.,(Article 23 (2)	Article 39 (d)
3.	Right to just and Favourable Remuneration (Article 23 (3)	Article 43
4.	Right to Rest to Leisure (Article 24 (1)	Article 43

5.	Right of Everyone and a Standard of Living adequate for him and his family (Article 25 (1)	Article 39 (a) & 47
6.	Right to Education and Free Education in Elementary and Fundamental Stages (Article 26 (1)	Article 41 & 45
7.	Right to Proper Social Order (Article 28)	Article 38

Source: Shivani Sethi, "United Nations and Human Rights" *Third Concept*, January 2018, pp. 15-16.

Conclusion

We find all these provisions mentioned in Article 51A, such as dignity of women, respect to all people, common brotherhood amongst all people strive towards excellence in all spheres of individual and collective activity are very much related to the protection of human rights. At the same one can find the preamble, fundamental rights Directive Principles of State Policies and fundamental duties try to protect and promote human rights as enshrined in the Universal Declaration of Human Rights and the International Covenant on Civil and Political Rights and the Convention on the Rights of the Child. On the other hand we can say that the Charter of the United Nations and the Charter of Human Rights inspired the framers of Indian Constitution. Hence, the government of India has been striving hard to implement the various provisions of Human Rights mentioned on international bodies, not because it is mentioned certain rights in these Covenant, but also it is given in Indian Constitution. One can find a Symphonise Relationship between Indian Constitution and Human Rights.

Notes

1. Sapru Committee Report was published in 1945. In the early 1940s, India was dominated by the communal question raised between the Congress Party and the Muslim League. In order to resolve the communal problem and other issues, the Non-Party Conference was created under the chairmanship of Tej Bahadur Sapru, a well-known lawyer. He convened the first meeting in 1941. In its final report in 1945, the Non-Party Conference, prepared one section on Fundamental Rights, like freedom of speech, freedom of press, religious freedom and equality.Today it is known as Fundamental Rights and Directive Principles of State Policies, they are mentioned in Chapter III & IV of Indian Constitution.

2. N. K. Acharya (2009): *Constitution of India,* Asia Law House, Hyderabad, p. 1.
3. Word *'Secular'* was added in Indian Constitution according to the 42nd amendment Act, in 1976.
4. N K Acharya, (2009): *The Constitution of India*, Hyderabad: Asia Law House, pp. 13-44.
5. AIR 2005 SC 2677.
6. The Supreme Court, in a very important case Golakhnath *vs* State of Punjab, stated that any amendments that violated the provisions of Article 13 would be void. Again in another case in 1973, the Supreme Court in its landmark on *Kesavananda Bharati vs. State of Kerala* held that the Parliament under the Indian Constitution is not supreme, in that it cannot change the *basic structure* of the constitution. See Details in Keshwanand Bharati vs State of Kerala, AIR 1973 SC 1461 and also in Minerva Mills Ltd., *vs* Union of India, AIR 1980, SC, 1789.
7. See Keshwanand Bharati *vs* Government of Kerala case 1973, S. C. 1461.
8. Right to property was one among fundamental Rights. According 44th Constitutional Amendment Act 1978. It is no more a fundamental Right anymore. Article 31 (1) has been taken out of Part III, and made a separate Article, viz., 300A which says: No person shall be deprived of his property save by authority of law.
9. See detail in the appendix 1 page no. 155.
10. See Second Paragraph of the Preamble of the Charter of the United Nations and paragraph 3 of Article 1.
11. See, International Covenant on the Elimination of All Forms of Racial Discrimination 1965, Article 1.
12. See details, Peoples Union for democratic Rights *Vs* Union of India AIR 1982 SC. 1473.
13. A. I. R. 1978 S. C. 597.
14. Pathumma *v* State of Kerala, (1978) 2 SCC 1.
15. *Ibid.* at 658.
16. Inserted by Constitution (Eighty-sixth Amendment) Act, 2002 dated 12/12/2002.
17. A.D.M. Jabalpur *vs* Shiv Kant Shukla, A.I.R. 1976 S.C. 1207.
18. https://www.theleaflet.in/un-special-rapporteurs-express-concerns-over-uapa The Leaflet 18 May 2020.
19. The right to propagate means each member of every religion has a right to spread disseminate the tenets of his religion, but it would not include the right to convert another because each man has the same freedom of conscience guaranteed by that very provision Art 25(1), see details Stanislaus *vs* State of M. P., A.I.R 1977 S.C. 908.

20. The word 'Secular' was added to the Indian Constitution Preamble according to 42nd Amendment Act 1976. The word secular means that the State protects all religions equally and does not itself uphold any religion as State religion.
21. This clause was inserted in the Constitution by the 44th Amendment Act 1978, Sec. w.e.f. 20.06.1979.
22. Olga Tellis *vs* Bombay Municipal Corporation, (1985) 3 SCC 545 at 573.
23. Now there has been a Constitutional amendment in 2009, which provides Right to education to all from the age group of 6 to 14. It has become a fundamental Right now and new article has been added as article 21-A. The Right of Children to Free and Compulsory Education Act or Right to Education Act is an Act of the Parliament of India enacted on August 4, 2009, which describes the modalities of the importance of free and compulsory education for children between 6 to 14 years in India.

2

Minorities and Human Rights: A Symbiotic Relationship

Introduction

Technically minorities are those who are in some sense, in a minority in a particular area of a particular system. In most usages minorities are thought of as having common positive identities, rather being united in their opposition to the majority. The politically important sense of minority is that it is a group in society, which has a set of common interests and beliefs over a wide set of issues, which marks it out as needing, deserving or even being given special treatment that the majority of citizens do not have. The most common politically-important minorities are racial, religious or ethnic groups in a society who are seen as suffering across a broad spectrum of disadvantages and needing special legal protection and positive discrimination or affirmative action.

Minorities form an integral part of Indian Political System and can be dispassionately studied and dissected from multiple standpoints. Minorities of different types do acquire an independent and autonomous profile of their own due to their distinct uniqueness. It pivots around demography, migration, geography, culture, religion, ethnicity and language. These aforementioned factors impinge on mainstream society and national polity, as India is a multi-ethnic, multi-cultural, multi-religious and multi-tribal society with secularism as its main political creed. It has a subtle and nuanced international dimension, too.

The term minority refers to groups and sections of society which in demographic sense are less in number than the numerically larger majority community. Religion-wise, in India, the Hindus constitute the majority while other religious groups like- the Muslims, Sikhs, Parsis, Jains, Anglo-Indians, Buddhists and Christians are deemed as religious minorities (See Table 1 Composition of Religions). Be that as it may, in dramatic parlance one could say there is also a sub-plot within a main plot. Christian community in Kerala though a minority yet demography wise, the Christians form a good sizable community. In contrast to this in Jammu and Kashmir, the Christian community is very miniscule in terms of numbers. There is another variation of this syndrome. In the state of Uttar Pradesh Muslims are in minority but in some constituencies and towns they are in majority. Like Mallapuran district in Kerala is a Muslim majority area.

Table 1: Composition of Religions in India****

	1981		1991		2001		2011	
Religious Group	**Total Million)**	**% of Total**	**Total (Million)**	**% of Total**	**Total (Million)**	**% of Total**	**Total (Million)**	**% of Total**
Hindus	549.7	82.6	672.6	82.41	827	80.5	966.3	79.8
Muslim	75.6	11.4	95.2	11.67	138	13.4	172.2	14.2
Christians	16.2	2.4	18.9	2.32	24	2.3	27.8	2.3
Sikh	13.1	2.0	16.3	1.99	19	1.9	20.8	1.7
Buddhists	4.7	0.7	6.3	0.77	7.9	0.8	8.4	0.7
Jains	3.2	0.5	3.4	0.41	4.2	0.4	4.5	0.4
Others*	2.8	0.4	3.5	0.43	6.6	0.6	7.9	0.7
Total	**665.3**	**100**	**81.62****	**100**	**1025.7**	**100**	**1207.9**	**100*****

Source: Census 1981, 1991 Paper I and 2001and 2011 (Religion)

* *Including unclassified persons*

** *Exclude Assam and Jammu and Kashmir 1981 data do not include Assam*

*** *Including Religion Not Stated 0.29 crores (0.2%) in 2011 census*

*** **2021 Census will be conducted in 2024*

The proportion of Hindu population to total population in 2011 has declined by 0.7 percentage point (PP); the proportion of Sikh population has declined by 0.2 PP and the Buddhist population has declined by 0.1 PP during the decade 2001-2011. The proportion of Muslim population to total population has increased by 0.8 PP. There has been no significant change in the proportion of Christians and

Jains. Again, if one speaks about the growth rate of population of different religious groups, we find there are substantial growth of few religious groups. The growth rate of population in the decade 2001-2011 was 17.7 percent. The growth rate of population of the different religious communities in the same period was as Hindus: 16.8 percent; Muslim: 24.6 percent; Christian: 15.5 percent; Sikh: 8.4 percent; Buddhist: 6.1 percent and Jain: 5.4 percent. The happiness and welfare of these minority communities ideally speaking should be the responsibility of the majority community who in view of their number have an in-build advantage in formation of any democratic government in power. As a result of this, the minority communities find their interests either being sidelined or being ignored by the government. The much condemned and castigated vote bank politics at times lead to situations where artificially contrived communal conflict is viewed as a weapon to capture political power. Pandit Jawaharlal Nehru, the first Prime Minister of Independent India made some significant observations on the status of minorities. He said, *"Many of us are apt to imagine that India is particularly unfortunate in having to face a complicated problem of minorities and different communities. As a matter of fact, many other countries have faced and solved this problem."*

Be that as it may, if and when, any religious, cultural and linguistic minorities feel their minority rights is being trampled over by government or its agencies it immediately invokes those fundamental rights which is enshrined in the Constitution of India for remedial action. Articles like 29-30 of our Indian Constitution guarantees and safeguard minorities' rights. The constitution speaks of three minorities based on religion, culture and language. Though strictly speaking sexual minority rights is also gradually coming on the centre stage of public attention.

To avoid conceptual semantics or obfuscation a concise-cum-precise definition of minorities is imperative for rigorous analysis of minority problem and one can quote Myron Weiner in this context. He says "*A people who do not share what they regard as the Central symbols of the society invariably view themselves as a minority.*"[1] From this definition of the American scholar the interface between minority-majority status is after all a matter of self-ascription.

So, the element of flexibility in usage of the term takes care of various nuances of the minority syndrome. What is a majority from one perspective is a minority from another. For example, Muslims, the second largest religious minority of the country is in majority in Jammu and Kashmir while in Nagaland or Gujarat they do not demography-wise qualify for the same status of the former. Likewise, Christians are in majority in Nagaland, Meghalaya and Mizoram but in Punjab they are in microscopic minority. In spite of religious minority, in India we have also linguistic minority. Next part of this chapter would be on linguistic minority and its legal status.

Linguistic Minority

Another dimension of the problem of minority is language-specific, when a person leaves his/her States and moves into another State he/she has transited to an area where he/she falls into the linguistic minority group.[2] There will be less percentage of people who will speak that language. In the name of preserving their language, people may start schools/colleges for those students. In order to preserve their language, school/college management can reserve 50 percent seat for linguistic minorities. They come under the category of linguistic minority.

Table 2: First, Second and Third languages by number of speakers in India (Census, 2011)

	First Language Speakers		Second Language Speakers	Third Language Speakers	Total Speakers	
Language	Figure	% of total population			Figure	% of Total population
Hindi	528347,193	43.63	139207,180	24,160,696	691,347,193	57.09
Bengali	97,237,669	8.03	9,037,222	1,008,088	107,237,669	8.85
Marathi	83026,680	6.86	12,923,626	2,966,019	99,026,680	8.18
Telugu	81,127,740	6.70	11,946,414	1,001,498	94,127,740	7.77
Tamil	69,026,881	5.70	6,992,253	956,335	77,026,881	6.36
Gujarati	55,492,554	4.58	4,035,489	1,007,912	60,492,554	4.99
Urdu	50,772,631	4.19	11,055,287	1,096,428	62,772,631	5.18
Kannada	43,706,512	3.61	14,076,355	993,989	58,706,512	4.84
Odia	37,521,324	3.10	4,972,151	31,525	42,551,324	3.51
Malayalam	34,838,819	2.88	499,188	195,885	35,538,819	2.93
Punjabi	33,124,726	2.74	2,300,000	720,000	36,074,726	2.97
Assamese	15,311,351	1.26%	7,488,153	740,402	23,539,906	1.94%

Source: Census of India, 2011.

However, some sociologists define 'minority' differently. According to the International Encyclopedia of Sociology, "Minority groups are defined by their powerlessness relative to other groups in a society, and majority groups are the reverse: They dominate other groups".[3] Anthropologists Charles Wagely and Marvin Harris have put forward a widely accepted definition of the term "minority group". In Minorities in the New World: Six Case Studies (1958), they argued that five characteristics identify these groups. First, they are relatively powerless compared with members of dominant group. Secondly, this fact, along with their powerlessness, exposes them to unequal treatment. Third, their distinctive traits cause minority groups to become self-conscious social units. Fourth, an established rule of descent exists for transmitting membership in minority groups across generations. Fifth, members of minority groups by and large tend to marry within their groups.[4]

One cannot underestimate how much minority problem hovers and revolves around the independent dynamic variable of language. It may not be out of place to mention that the Constitution of India has recognised 22 languages, which are spoken by most of the Indian population. Ninety percent of population speaks one of these 22 languages. The demand for inclusion of languages like Nepali, Manipuri (Meitei or Meetei language a Tibeto-Burman language spoken predominantly in Manipur, they are in majority) and Konkani has been made in post-1990 period. These three languages were included in the Eighth Schedule of the Constitution of India in 1992 by the Seventy First Amendment Act 1992. In 2003, four more languages were added: *Bodo, Maithili, Dogri and Santhali*. (See details in Table 3, with decadal variant) If one studies carefully the decadal difference of languages between 2001-2011 one finds that that there is a decline of various states languages. There is an increase in Gujarati language. To keep its secular credentials shining, the Central and State governments have left no stone unturned to protect and safeguard various scripts and languages from extinction from lack of usage. But state patronage and support has not succeeded in extinction of some dialects and scripts. More so, the scripts could not be put in systematic linguistic format.

Table 3: Languages of India*-number of speakers in three decades

Sl. No.	Language	1991 Census		2001 Census		2011 Census	
		Speaker	Percentage	Speaker	Percentage	Speaker	Percentage
1.	Hindi	329,518,087	39.29	422,048,624	41.1	528,347,193	43.63
2.	Bengali	69,595,738	8.30	83,369,769	8.11	97,237,669	8.03
3.	Marathi	62,481,681	7.45	71,936,894	6.99	83,026,680	6.86
4.	Telgu	66,017,615	7.87	74,002,856	7.19	81,127,740	6.70
5.	Tamil	53,006,368	6.32	60,793,814	5.91	69,026,881	5.70
6.	Gujarati	40,673,814	4.85	46,091,617	4.48	55,492,554	4.58
7.	Urdu	43,406,932	5.18	51,536,111	5.01	50,772,631	4.19
8.	Kannada	32,753,676	3.91	37,924,011	3.69	43,706,512	3.61
9.	Oriya	28,061,313	3.35	33,017,446	3.21	37,521,324	3.10
10.	Malayalam	30,377,176	3.62	33,066,392	3.21	34,838,819	2.88
11.	Punjabi	23,378,744	2.79	29,102,477	2.83	33,124,726	2.74
12.	Assamese	13,079,696	1.56	13,168,484	1.28	15,311,351	1.26
13.	Maithili	7,766,921	0.926	12,179,122	1.18	13,583,464	1.12
14.	Santhali	5,216,325	0.622	6,469,600	0.63	7,368,192	0.61
15.	Kashmiri	N. A.	N. A.	5,527,698	0.54	6,797,587	0.56
16.	Nepali	2,076,645	0.248	2,871,749	0.28	2,926,168	0.24
17.	Sindhi	2,122,848	0.253	2,535,485	0.25	2,772,264	0.23

18.	Dogri	N. A.	N. A.	2,282,589	0.22	2,596,767	0.21
19.	Konkani	1,760,607	0.210	2,489,015	0.24	2,256,502	0.19
20.	Bodo	1,221,881	0.146	1,350,478	0.13	1,482,929	0.12
21.	**Manipuri	1,270,216	0.15	1,466,705	***0.14	1,761,079	0.15
22.	Sanskrit	49,736	0,01	14,135	0.001	24,821	0.002

Source: Census of India, 1991, 2001 and 2011.

N. A.: Not Available; N: Negligible * Figures for 18 of the 22 Languages. Speakers of BODO: 12,21,881(1991Census); DOGRI: 21,05,000 (1991 IMA); SANTHALI: 52, 16,325 (1991 Census);

MAITHILI: 2, 20, 00,000 (1981 Census).

By the 71st Amendment to the Constitution, Konkani, Manipuri and Nepali were added to the list in 1992.

In 2003, four more languages were added: *Bodo, Maithili, Dogri and Santhali.*

** Excludes figures of Paomata, Mao-Maram and Purul sub-divisions of Senapati district of Manipur for 2001.

*** The percentage of speakers of each language for 2001 has been worked out on the total population of India excluding the population of Mao-Maram, Paomata and Purul subdivisions of Senapati district of Manipur due to cancellation of census results.

2021 Census will be conducted in 2024.

Another very important facet of minority landscape is the existence of various cultural and tribal and aboriginal groups in the country who are interested to maintain and preserve their separate cultural and tribal identity. Meitie and Meitei Pangals in Manipur want that their community be considered as Scheduled Tribe in order to preserve their culture and language.[5] And by no long shot the Constitution has not kept it out of its orbit of concern and protection. Interestingly enough the policy of Central and State government is continuation of the pre-1947 view of many outstanding British anthropologists, archeologists and ethnographers. To give few random examples would be J. H. Hutton, J. S. Mill and Verrier Elwin.

The concept and usage of the term minority is not of recent historical vintage. It goes back to time immemorial as people of different religious, cultural and linguistic groups coexisted under dispensation of various empires and political entities. So, it is not surprising that the term was in wide currency during pre- and post-1947 period of Indian History. During the time of Constituent Assembly debates, one notices various representatives of minority groups spoke on behalf of their own people. In fact, the Sikh representative Hukum Singh and his colleague due to their dissatisfaction did not affix their signatures on the document prepared by the Constituent Assembly. Incidentally Sardar Hukum Singh became speaker of *Lok Sabha* (1962-67).

The present demand for safeguards and protection of Scheduled Castes (also called before Depressed Class) had a long history dating Montague-Chelmsford reform of 1919. Dr B R Ambedkar had been closely involved in this struggle for giving Scheduled Caste people some solid statutory safeguard. His forceful advocacy in Round Table Conference called by the then British Prime Minister Ramsay Macdonald is well-known fact. So, it is no matter of surprise that the Constitution which the country received on January 26, 1950, Dr Ambedkar saw to it that Scheduled Caste people have iron-clad guarantee in form of reservation, i.e., legislative, employment and educational field.

Though he deserves rightful appreciation for drafting the Constitution, he had some apprehension about his own handiwork. He lamented the fact that the Constitution has given India political democracy, but not social and economic democracy. He preferred participatory democracy instead of parliamentary democracy.[6]

Minorities and Constituent Assembly Debates

It would be appropriate at this stage to go back to the Constituent Assembly debates for better appreciation of the question of minority rights, which evoked sharp debates and lengthy discussion amongst varied participants belonging to different political and religious affiliation. During the debates, there were general agreements for the provisions for minority's safeguards in the new Constitution. The discussion on the 'minority' was much more prolonged, controversial and at times heated than the discussion on the 'backward classes.' After protracted debate and discussion consensus was reached on various contentious issues relating to minority safeguards and of backward classes. For resolution of this issue, on January 24, 1947, the Constituent Assembly appointed an Advisory Committee on Minorities with Sardar Vallabhai Patel as the Chairman. This committee after exhaustive discussions submitted its reports on August 8, 1947. The recommendations in the Report "*Where there were not unanimous, were taken by very large majorities composed substantially of members belonging to minority communities themselves.*" This report recommended the abolition of separate electorates, but was in favour of reservation of seats in the legislatures for minorities on the basis of their population.

As Sardar Patel reported, the Indian Christian Community under the leadership of Dr. H. C. Mookerjee, the Vice President of the Constituent Assembly and also Chairman of the Minority sub-committee (a Christian Member), Ms. Rajkumari Amrit Kaur (a Christian representative in sub-committee), Rev. Fr. Jerome D'Souza, S. J. (Madras: General), Rev. J. J. M. Nichols-Roy (Assam: General), Mr. C. E. Gibbon (C. P. & Berar: General) and Mr. Frank Anthony had from the beginning opposed any reservation in the constitution and had voluntarily given up all reservation for themselves.[7]

A caveat is well in order that the Indian Christian and Anglo-Indian Christian members of the Constituent Assembly had no easy walkover in fight for minority rights of Christians, as lot of members had serious reservation over the question of conversion and propagation of the religion particularly to tribal and poorer section of society. But all said and done the Advisory Committee, however, "thought it necessary to allay the apprehensions of the minorities at the time", and recommended reservation under joint electorate.[8] These recommendations of Advisory Committee were finally accepted by the Constituent Assembly, and Sardar Patel commented that "practically unanimously and a general sense of appreciation was expressed by the minorities when these proposals were accepted."[9] A reading of this Report on Minority Rights and the discussion, which it spawned, clearly shows that at this stage Scheduled Castes were regarded as one of the minority groups.[10]

Mr. V. I. Muniswami Pillai said that the Scheduled Castes constitute one-sixth of total population and they are to be considered minority community. As a follow-up action a list of the minority communities was prepared and was submitted to Constituent Assembly. It was agreed that the Scheduled Caste community is one of the minorities. But towards the penultimate stage of the discussion on the Report there was a change, which came in the form of an amendment moved by K. M. Munshi of Bombay and Shibban Lal Saksena of United Provinces. It was concerned with the Hindu status of the Scheduled Castes and was accepted by the house without much discussion. At that moment the minority communities Muslim, Sikh and Christians-either did not realise the significance of the amendment or preferred to be silent about it. The Scheduled Castes themselves seemed to have accepted the implications of the amendment.

The amendment, in effect, meant three things: (i) the Scheduled Castes were separated from other religious minorities, (ii) they were made a part of the Hindu Community; and (iii) they were given all the same rights and benefits provided for minorities. Later, when reservations for religious minorities, were abolished, the rights and benefits for Scheduled Castes would still remain intact.

Mr. K. M. Munshi of Bombay explained the object of this amendment by stating that the word Minorities as used in the international law referred to racial and linguistic minorities. He felt that the extension of the term to refer to the Scheduled Castes as Sir Samuel Hoare (the Secretary of State for India who later became Foreign Secretary) did in Government of India Act, 1935, was "mischievous extension of the term." He stated that the "*Harijans* are part and parcel of Hindu community, and the safeguards are given to them to protect their rights only till they are completely absorbed in the Hindu community."[11] Surprisingly, neither Dr B. R. Ambedkar nor any other member of the Scheduled Castes objected to the explanation. The members of other minorities were silent. The amendments were moved and passed without much ado. The problem would surface when reservation for minority would be abolished and only those for the Scheduled Castes and Scheduled Tribes and Anglo-Indian would remain intact.[12]

All those who originally belonged to the scheduled castes but who accepted a religion different from other than Hinduism would then be automatically excluded from benefits of such programmes. There were some members in the Advisory Committee who were in favour of dropping all reservation. At the same time scheduled castes members request that reservations in their case be continued for ten years. The Advisory Committee, Sardar Patel reported, almost unanimously accepted this request.[13] Under these circumstances the Advisory Committee thought it fit to reconsider the whole issue of reservation for minorities. Sufficient time was given to members of minority communities to reflect on the new proposal to establish reservation for minorities and "to gauge public opinion among the people". However, it was accepted that the reservation for Scheduled Castes to be continued for ten years beginning from May 1949.[14] Even this is being extended every ten years.

But the Sikh community put forth another demand that the scheduled caste converts to Sikhism in East Punjab to be treated as Scheduled Castes. They argued these groups in East Punjab- *Mazhabis, Ramdasis, Kabirpanthis and Sikligars*- who were recent converts and who were originally Scheduled Castes Hindus suffered from the same disabilities as scheduled castes Hindu suffered.

The reaction to the demand of the Sikh Communities from Sardar Patel, who masterminded the whole Minorities Committee Report, was unfavourable and the issue resurfaced in later years.[15] Sardar Patel who wholeheartedly supported the demand of the Hindu Scheduled Castes was clearly irked by the demand of the Sikhs for the same status for Scheduled Castes converts to Sikhism. "These converts are not Scheduled Castes", he said and ought not to be Scheduled Castes; because in the Sikh religion, "there is no such thing as untouchability or any classifications or difference of classes".

According to Sardar Patel the Sikhs were asking for this 'privilege' because if these Scheduled Castes who have been converted to Sikhism are not given the same benefits as the scheduled castes have been, there is a possibility of their reverting to the Hindu Scheduled Castes and merging along with them. He "urged upon them (Sikhs) strongly not to lower their religion to such a pitch as to really fall to a level where for a mass of pottage you really give up the substance of religion". Sardar Patel also reported that there was considerable opposition to the Sikh demand from the Hindu Scheduled Castes, *"who had a justifiable fear complex that if they agree to this, or if the House accepts this position, there is really a danger of forcible conversion from their class to the Scheduled Castes Sikh"*...He appealed to the majority community "*to create by its generosity a sense of confidence in the minorities*". In the same breath he appealed to the minority communities, *"to rise to the situation that is demanded from all of us, and create an atmosphere in which sooner these classifications disappear the better"*. He asked the Scheduled Castes Hindus *"not to resent or grudge the concession that is made in the case of the Sikh..."*

Pandit Jawaharlal Nehru said that the reservation to minorities is to be abolished.[16] He also said that "*It is a notion which means not only discarding something that was evil, but turning back upon it and determining with all our strength that we shall pursue a path which is considered fundamentally good for every part of the Nation*". Nehru said that I try to look upon the problem not in the sense of a religious minority, but rather in the sense of helping backward groups in the country. Nehru's aversion to the use of the term religious minority and his preference to use the term backward group meant that the discussion was centered on a particular section of the people who were defined as Hindus and from whom others were excluded merely on the basis of their profession of another religion. This problem would become much more acute when later the President of the Indian Republic would declare profession of Hinduism a pre-condition to be a member of a Scheduled Caste. The final Report on Minority Rights etc. was thus accepted by the Constituent Assembly with some minor additions. In the Presidential Order of 1950, Sikhs were not included in the Scheduled Castes list. But after Independence, the discussion on the inclusion of Sikh community resurfaced with much passion and tenacity.

The third paragraph of the Presidential Order 1950 used religion as a criterion to define the Scheduled Castes and based on this criterion it also added that only those backwards (socially, educationally and economically), who will profess Hindu religion will enjoy this status. So based on this criterion all other people professing Islam, Sikhism, Buddhism, Christianity and others were left out. But in 1956 and 1990, the third paragraph of the Presidential Order 1950 was amended by the Parliament to extend the constitutional benefits to *Dalit* Sikhs and *Dalit* Buddhist along with *Dalit* Hindu respectively.[17]

In this whole process of debates on the provisions for the Constitutional concession, the Muslims, Christians and Jains Minorities were kept away from these statutory concessions, though they were given all protection by the Constitution to live in dignity without any fear.[18] To ensure the peaceful coexistence of minority groups, the Constitution of India 1950 provides in Articles 12-35 a comprehensive framework to safeguard the rights of Indian citizen. Article 14 declares "*the State shall not deny to any person equality before law or equal protection of the laws within the territory of India*". Article 15 states that "*the State shall not discriminate against any citizen on grounds only of religion, race, caste, sex, place of birth or any of them*". Article 16 guarantees equality of opportunity in matters of public employment. Article says that all persons are equally entitled to freedom of conscience and right freely to profess, practice and propagate religion. Article 26 guarantees the freedom to manage religious affairs. Article 27 provides an additional protection to religious activity by exempting funds appropriated towards the promotion or maintenance of any particular religion from the payment of taxes. Article 28 prohibits religious instruction in any educational institution wholly maintained out of State funds whether such instruction is given by the State or by any other body.

Under Articles 29 and 30, certain cultural and educational rights of the minorities are guaranteed. Section (1) Article 29 guarantees the right of any section of the citizens residing in any part of the country having a distinct language, script or culture of its own, to conserve the same. Section (2) prohibits any discrimination based only on religion, race, caste, language or any of them in the matter of administration to state or state aided educational institutions. Section (1) of Article 30 provides that *"all minorities, whether based on religion or language, shall have the right to establish and administer educational institutions of their choice"*. According to Section (2), the State shall not, in granting aid to educational institutions, discriminate against any educational institutions on the ground that it is under the management of a minority whether based on religion or language.

Protection to Linguistic Minority

The Constitution provides protection to linguistic minority also. Article 350-A imposes a duty on the State to endeavour to provide facilities for instruction in the mother tongue at the primary stage of education to children belonging to linguistic minority. Article 350-B empowers the President to appoint a special officer to investigate all matters relating to the safeguards provided for linguistic minority under the Constitution.

Besides Constitutional provisions for protection of minorities enshrined in the Constitution of 1950, the Janata Government headed by Prime Minister Morarji Desai in 1978 had constituted a National Commission for Minorities.[19] This Commission was asked to find out various vexatious cases, which had bearing on religious minorities of India. The Commission was instructed to submit to Parliament its report every year. A new phenomenon emerged as the restive *Dalit* Christians were seething with discontentment for being out of the purview of reservation benefits. Their contention had been that though they had converted to Christianity they suffer from the same social, educational and economic disabilities as before. Belatedly, the Christian community in general and newly converted *Dalit* Christians in particular launched their protest at the highest corridors of powers for necessary justice to be given to them. In context of this the Catholic Bishops' Conference of India met at Tiruchirappalli on January 4-14, 1982 considered the question of caste and its baneful efforts both on society at large and within the Church. Similarly, Church of North India had noted the cause of *Dalit* Christian in its conclave of October 6-10, 1992 and observed that the fundamental Rights of *Dalit* Christians should be restored, which they have lost through the Presidential Order of 1950. They all asserted that *Dalit* Christians should be included in the List of Scheduled Castes.[20] An attempt was made from 1991 to 1994 to introduce a bill making provision for reservation to *Dalit* Christians. Narayans Swamy introduced a private member's bill recommending the amendment of the Constitution (Scheduled Castes Orders) so as to include the *Dalit* Christians under purview. But there was no reason to deny them the rights on the ground of conversion. This bill could not see the light of the day.

Again, in a Cabinet note dated March 1996, Welfare Minister had proposed to introduce for the inclusion of *Dalit* Christian in Scheduled Caste list. The Cabinet approved this proposal at its meeting and then the Constitution Amendment Bill (Scheduled Caste) was prepared. Although the bill was listed for introduction as a supplementary item in the Lok Sabha on March 1996, it could not be introduced. Following the adjournment of Parliament, the cabinet decided that an Ordinance be issued in this regard. An ordinance was proposed to the President of India, but was not promulgated.[21]

On August 2022, the Supreme Court asked the Centre to clarify governmental stand in the matter on the petition filed by the National Council of Dalit Christians and others on the question of list *Dalit* Christian in the Scheduled list. The Central Government in a written reply said that, "The Constitution (Scheduled Caste) Order 1950 was based on historical data which clearly established that no such backwardness or oppression was ever faced by members of Christian or Islamic Society."[22] Though Justice Ranganath Misra Commission for Religious and Linguistic Minorities had proposed providing reservation to *Dalits* who converted to Christianity and Islam.[23] The Central Government also said that *Dalit* who are converted to Christianity and Islam, should not be allowed, since they do not suffer from untouchability. Again on April 12, 2023, when Justice S K Kaul, was presiding a three-judge bench, questioned while hearing petition, seeking Scheduled Caste status for those who converted to Christianity and Islam, "Can caste be imputed to other religions when the religion does not provide for any such discrimination in its structure..."[24] In the meanwhile, the Tamil Nadu Chief Minister M K Stalin has moved a resolution in the State Assembly seeking to bring *Dalit* Christians under the ambit of reservation for scheduled castes (SC). This resolution states that *Dalits* who converted to Christianity continue to face untouchability and caste atrocities.[25]

Christian leaders and lay people cutting across the Roman Catholic-Protestants divide with benefit of hindsight have developed some doubt over the wisdom of Christian representatives like Rev. Jerome D'Souza, S. J., Dr. H. C. Mukherjee and Ms. Rajkumari Amrit Kaur during Constituent Assembly Debates of so cavalierly forgone reservation benefits which was there for mere asking. The problem of Dalit Christian is not a new phenomenon, though it has come on the center stage of politics recently. Long list of Christian leaders, including men and women have carved a niche for themselves in Indian politics and society, yet sadly speaking no one championed the cause of Dalit Christians. The roster of names is very imposing. The names are like Dr. H. C. Mukherjee, Mr. W. C. Bonarjee, Mrs. Nellie Sen Gupta, Fr. Jerome D'Souza, S. J., Mr. Frank Anthony, Mr. C. E. Gibbon and others. In hindsight we can very well understand why the honourable members of the Constituent Assembly for its inclusion did not raise the cause of *Dalit* Christians. Firstly, none of them belonged to *Dalit* Christian community and in first flush of idealism of the time they were just carried away in their enthusiasm. Had some one like Dr. Ambedkar been there representing *Dalit* Christians, things may have been different. Further, the leaders of the Christian community neither felt the need to have a Christian caucus group in Parliament or the formation of a political party to strengthen and safeguard the rights and privileges of Christian community as such.

Minority and Demand for a Separate State

Many a times, the problems of minorities led to the demands of separate State,[26] yet part of the Indian Union. At times shades of forming an independent State had been also there. Proud of their ancient cultural and linguistic greatness Tamils of South India radiating from the metropolis of Madras flirted with the idea of carving out a new independent State of Tamil speaking people. The Malayalam-speaking areas of Malabar was joined Trawancore Cochin to form a new State of Kerela in consonance with the norm adopted by State of Reorganisation Commission of 1955. The *malayam*-speaking area Malabar to Travencore Cochin was converted to Kerala. This division was based on language. Sikhs agitation for a separate Punjabi *Suba* was also viewed by many of its proponents to serve as a launching-pad for creation of a new full-fledged State of Khalistan. This again was on the basis on religion and language. From PEPSU, three States were trifurcated and emerged as Punjab, Himachal Pradesh and Haryana. There has already been demand for a *Bodo* State be carved out of Assam. For preservation of their tribal identity the people of Jharkhand succeeded in the end to have new State of their own severing its ties with undivided Bihar in 2002. Similarly, in order to preserve the tribal culture and language, tribal people demanded for new State and thereby a new State, Chhattisgadh was created. The Sikhs and the *Gurkhas* under the mantle of extreme leaders espoused the cause of their respective communities either for a separate State or more regional autonomy in the federal framework. Jagjit Singh Chauhan or Subash Ghising to pick random examples were of the same ilk. New Delhi had to bend backwards to accommodate the demands of these leaders through various means. Justice R. S. Sarkaria Commission was constituted in the context of Sikh demand to go into the entire gamut of Centre-State relationship in a federal Constitution. The Gurkha Supremo, Ghising managed to get Development Council for *Gurkhas* at Dajeeling and inclusion of Nepali language in VIII Scheduled of the Constitution of India. Language issue was raked up by *Shetkari Sanghatan* leader of Maharashtra Sharad Joshi for transfer of Marathi speaking Belgam from the control of Karnataka to the Maharashtra. Ethnic tensions between the hill communities and Meiteis in Manipur existed from the time of the erstwhile kingdom with the advent of the Naga national movement in the 1950s, and the call for an independent Naga Nation. In the 1990s, as the NSCN-IM (National Council of Nagaland, led by Isak Chishi and Thuingaleng Muivah) had pushed harder for Self-Determination and at the same time the Kuki-Zomi groups began to militarise, and the Kukis launched their own movement for 'Kukiland'. After sometime, Kuki-Zoma demanded for a state within India, not a separate national homeland.[27] Kukis wants to have a separate administration in the form of a Union Territory for the Kuki-dominated districts or other political safeguard in Manipur.

There was a demand for splitting Bombay into Gujarat and Maharashtra. Despite Pandit Jawaharlal Nehru's preference for a composite one State of Bombay, the linguistic chauvinism led to the formation of two entities Maharashtra and Gujarat in1960. And to top it Bombay became part of Maharashtra and for his strong espousal Union Finance Minister C.D. Deshmukh resigned from the Cabinet in 1956.

The geographical map of the entire country was fashioned on the basis of recommendation of States Reorganisation Committee under the Chairmanship of Fazal Ali in 1955. It recommended that the Indian Union be geographically reconstituted on criteria of language and as a result of it the Union comprised sixteen States and three centrally administered areas. As a result of it gradually the number of States rose to twenty-five.[28] Till today we have 28 States in India. Then ruling Congress party thus redeemed its promise made in Nagpur session of the Congress Party in December 1920 that independent India would be divided into States on the criterion of language. The political profile also changed as a result of it. Each linguistic State catapulted political leaders who represented the regional aspirations of the people. The common glue between States leaders and State people was language.

There was one important caveat to be borne in mind. Though the juggernaut of linguistic division of the country rolled on, one has to remember that India after all is a multi-lingual, multi-racial, multi-ethnic and multi-religious country. Because of this ground reality each linguistically carved State had within its territorial borders many minuscule linguistic religious, racial, minorities and whose total welfare was on the shoulders of leadership and people of the States. As mentioned before a sexual minority has to still gather momentum to wrest some rights for their decent and dignified existence in a society which views them as moral lepers or pariahs.

Conclusion

Notwithstanding these developments and political constants,

legitimate demands of linguistic minorities fell short of their optimum satisfaction. Unfortunately, political fall-outs at times became inevitable. It oscillated between over zealous concern for well being of linguistic minorities to benign neglect like the swings of a pendulum.

The bottom line remains that when nations like former Yugoslavia and the old USSR could unravel the Indian Republic has survived as one entity with no secession or dissolution of any sort. Minorities whether religious or linguistic, in India enjoy their rights in every states. They may be numerically less in some states, but still enjoy their rights as enshrined in Indian Constitution. Despite many hiccups and moments of crises, minority rights and human rights is given due place and significance in the Indian nation State. There is a symbiotic relationship between minority and human rights.

Notes

1. Myron Weiner, Indian Paradox. (New Delhi) 1989. p. 42.
2. *Ibid*, p. 41.
3. See, International Encyclopedia of Sociology, Vol. 2, 1995, p. 834.
4. *Ibid.*
5. Sukriti Barua, "Behind Manipur Flare-up, Tribal anger, HC order," *Indian Express*, May 5, 2023.
6. Dr B. R. Ambedkar, *State and Minority* (Hindi) 1947, p. 1.
7. H. C. Mookherjee, speaking at the Constituent Assembly on August 27, 1947 said: "I am a member of the minority community myself and I feel proud that the community, of which I am a member, has decided to give up all special privileges…" for detail see Vol. 5. 208, Constituent Assembly Debate.
8. Rev. Fr. Jerome D' Souza, S. J. remarked that reservation was made necessary because the Congress Party had from the beginning advocated joint electorates and that it would have been a breach of promise to give up reservation at that time. *I do not deny that there are dissident voices*. But we have in touch with our people up and down the country and I think I can say with certainty that as far as the Christian community is concerned, in the light of letters received and the public expression of opinion which we have heard, India as a whole is behind Dr. Mookherjee in his decision that there should be no reservation of seats.
9. For detail, see Constituent Assembly Debate, Vol. 8, p. 270.
10. On the problems of minority, Sardar Patel said, "We wish to make it clear, however, that our general approach to the whole problem of minorities is

that the state would be so run that they should stop feeling oppressed by the mere fact that they are minorities and on the contrary, they feel that they have as honourable a part to play in the national life as any other section of the community. Also see the views of Dr. P. S. Deshmukh and V. I. Munswami Pillai from Madras in the Constituent Assembly Debates, Vol. 5, pp. 225, and 270-272.

11. For detail, see Constituent Assembly Debates, Vol. 5, p. 227.
12. The Government of India Act 1935 provided due weightage to the various communities, classes and interests in the two Houses of the Federal Legislature. The members of the Legislative Assembly were to be indirectly elected by the Provincial Legislative Assemblies on the basis of the principle of proportional representation with single transferable vote. Community-wise the 250 seats of the Legislative Assembly were distributed thus: General seats 105 including 19 Scheduled Castes seats; Muslim seats 82; Sikh seats 6; Anglo-Indian seats 4; Europeans 8; Indian Christians 11; representatives of Commerce and Industry 11; representatives of Labour 10; representatives of Landholders 7; and women 9 seats. There were 11 Provinces in India during that time.
13. See Constituent Assembly Report, Vol. 8, p. 270.
14. Now the reservation for the scheduled castes and scheduled tribes is being extended every ten years. It has been taken as vote bank for ruling party.
15. This was later (1956) changed by the Parliament to "Hinduism or Sikhism'. "Provided that every member of the *Ramdasi, Kabirpanthi, Mazhabi or Sikligar* caste resident in Punjab or the Patiala and East Punjab States Union shall, in relation to that State, be deemed to be a member of the Scheduled Castes whether he professes the Hinduism or the Sikh religion. Also see, the Presidential Order of 1950.
16. See Constituent Assembly Debates, Vol. 8, p. 320.
17. Neo-Buddhists are a religious group, which has come into existence in 1956 as a result of a wave of mass conversion of the lower castes under the leadership of Baba Saheb Ambedkar in Nagpur. On 14th Oct. a white garbed B. R. Ambedkar under the auspices of Burmese monk Sri Chnadramani in front of a half million of his political followers in the background of recitation in the *Pali* language of the ancient *Theravada* texts of Sri Lanka was initiated with *Navayana Diksha*. Up on conversion to Buddhism they became ineligible for statutory concession as they did belong to either fold of Hinduism or Sikhism. Neo-Buddhists are still fighting for their statutory concession as Scheduled Castes.
18. For details, See Prakash Louis, 'Ensuring Dignity of Minorities in India,' *Mainstream*, 17/1/ 2004.
19. The first Minorities Commission was set up in Uttar Pradesh in 1960. In the meanwhile in 1971 Bihar set up a multi-member Minorities commission. After U P and Bihar, Gujarat was third State to set a State Minorities

High Powered Committee consisting of a Chairman, a Vice-chairman and 22 members, including eight officials. In May 1992 the National Commission for Minorities Act, 1992 was enacted giving statutory status to the erstwhile Minorities Commission and thus making it a more effective body to safeguard the interest of Minorities. Also see appendix IV, National commission for minorities, in page 204.

20. See *North India Church Review* (a monthly Magazine of CNI) April 2005, p. 4.
21. S Lourduswamy, *Towards Empowerment of Dalit Christians: Equal Rights to All Dalits,* Centre for Dalit Studies, New Delhi, 2005, p. 113.
22. *Hitavada*, November 11, 2022, p. 1.
23. *Indian Express*, April 20, 2023, p. 13.
24. *Indian Express*, April 13, 2023, p. 1.
25. *Indian Express*, April 20, 2023, p. 13.
26. See Kunal Ghose and Vikash Kumar "Partition of Manipur, Greater Nagaland and Contrived Tangkhu Naga Identity," *Mainstream*, 6-12 May 2005, pp. 13- 18.
27. Esha Roy, "Manipur's ethnic faultlines," *Indian Express,* May 6, 2023, p. 12.
28. On 9th December 1953 a Commission was constituted under the Chairmanship of Fazle Ali to study the question of reorganisation of states on a linguistic basis. Other members were Hriday Nath Kunzru and K. M. Pannikkar. Today, India has 28 States including Chhattisgarh, Jharkhand, Uttaranchal.

3

B. R. Ambedkar: An Indefatigable Defender of Human Rights

Bhimrao Ramji Ambedkar was born as the fourteenth child of Mahar parents, Ramji and Bhimabai, on 14 April 1891 at Mhow, in present-day State of Madhya Pradesh. The Mahars are considered lower-caste and treated as low untouchables (Dalits) by higher caste Hindus. They are mainly found in the State of Maharashtra. The father and grandfather of Ambedkar served in the army and were of well-to-do family. But the stigma of being members of Mahar community caused their social oppression in a caste-ridden society.

Ambedkar had a bitter taste of discriminatory treatment due to his caste at an early age. He and his brother had to carry gunny bags to sit on inside the classroom because they were not allowed to sit on classroom chairs. They were denied drinking water facilities, and excluded from games and mixing with other children. Even teachers would not check their notebooks for fear of "pollution." Thus, sowed the seeds of discontentment about the Hindu social system in the life of Ambedkar.

He did his early education in Satara in Maharashtra State and then moved on to Bombay. In 1912, he passed his B. A. examination with distinction from the prestigious Elphinstone College with the scholarship and encouragement from the Maharaja of Baroda State.

In 1913, with a condition that he would serve the Baroda State for ten years, he was chosen by Maharaja of Baroda State for higher studies at Columbia University in the USA. This was followed with a trans-Atlantic shift to the United Kingdom where he studied at the University of London. While studying abroad, he mixed with students of various nationalities and races, which was an eyeopener for him.

He joined the Union Cabinet of Pandit Jawaharlal Nehru during the 1946-1951 period. He resigned on 27 September 1951 to protest the deferment of the discussion in the parliament of the Hindu Code Bill supposedly due to the coming 1952 elections. Ambedkar saw the Bill as a very important reform of Hindu law, with reform proposals on marriage, divorce, and monogamy.

Despite failing health, he plodded on with his advocacy for the cause of the Dalits. He came to Nagpur in October 1956 for his conversion to Buddhism and a couple of months thereafter on 8 December 1956 breathed his last.

Ambedkar's Movement for Human Rights

During the last decade of the nineteenth century, many Indian leaders born among the lower castes like Narayan Guru (1854-1928), Jotiba Phule (1827-1890), and Ramaswamy Naicker (1879-1973) launched massive struggles for the dignity of *Dalits* throughout India. Ambedkar was the most towering figure among these *Dalit* leaders.

In 1917, he joined the Baroda State Service after returning from his studies in the USA and the United Kingdom, as part of the terms of his scholarship agreement. He worked in the city of Baroda, the place of the ruling family of Gaikwad, which financed his studies abroad. He worked as secretary in the defense office of the Maharaja of Baroda State. However, despite his foreign education, he had to endure insults while at work due to his low caste origin. He was a victim of the cruel *dalit* discrimination. He suffered the ignominy of having document files hurled by peons at his face.[1]

He suffered the humiliating experience of not being served drinking water during official functions. At the officer's club, he had to sit in a corner and keep his distance from the other members belonging to higher castes. He also had difficulties in finding a rented house, as he was not allotted government bungalow. He stayed in an inn owned by Parsis (members of Zoroastrian religion). One morning, as he was getting ready to go to work, a dozen Parsis, all wielding sticks, rushed up to his room screaming that he had polluted the inn and insisted on his immediate departure. He begged them to let him stay for a week longer since he hoped to get his government bungalow by then. But they were obdurate. If they found him at the inn that evening, they said God help him. After spending much of the day in a public garden, Ambedkar, in utter frustration and disgust, left for Bombay by the 9 pm train.

These scorching incidents goaded Ambedkar to work for the protection of *dalit* rights and upliftment of the status of the *Dalits*. In 1924, he started legal practice in Bombay and founded the *Bahishkrit Hitkarni Sabha* (Depressed Class Institute) to uplift the *Dalits*. Henceforth, he started his movement and took the cause of the *Dalits*. He roused the *dali*t consciousness to fight for the eradication of *dalit* discrimination; to claim equality of treatment, status and opportunity; to equally enjoy all rights — civil, political, social and economic — and respect for the dignity of persons. He was considered a crusader for the human rights of the *Dalits* in India.[2]

The Hindu religious belief that "All human beings are not born equal" creates caste-based discrimination against the *Dalits* that leads to various forms of violence against them including public humiliation, torture, rape, beating and killing. Reacting to the values of Hinduism, Rabindranath Gore wrote,

> *We do not value Hinduism, we value human dignity...*
> *We want equal rights in the society. We will achieve*
> *them as far as possible while remaining within the*
> *Hindu fold or if necessary, by kicking away this*
> *worthless Hindu identity.*[3]

Ambedkar was a great supporter of women's liberation. He blamed the *verna* system, which has not only subjugated *Dalits* but also women. He questioned *Manu Smriti* (Laws of Manu), the law book (*Dharam-Shastra*) of Brahminic Hinduism and attributed to Manu, the legendary first man and law giver. *Manu Smriti* prescribed the Dharma of each Hindu, stating the obligations attached to his or her social class and stage of life. It was hostile to the interest of lower caste people and women. It prohibited re-marriage of widows. He felt that *Manu Smriti* was solely responsible for the downfall of Hindu women. He encouraged the *Dalits* to embrace Buddhism to liberate their own selves from Hindu subjugation. Hence, he fought for the right to choose ones' faith. After embracing Buddhism, Ambedkar said, "*Unfortunately for me I was born a Hindu Untouchable... I solemnly assure you I will not die as a Hindu.*" He practiced what he advocated and became a Buddhist in 1956.

He also wrote about the French revolution ideas of fraternity, liberty and equality. He thought that the French and Russian revolutions failed to realize all three ideas. He believed that they could not all be realised except through the way of the Buddha.[4]

Means and Ends for Struggle

He adopted various means to safeguard *dalit* rights. Ambedkar launched a movement against *dalit* discrimination by creating public opinion through his writings in several Periodicals such as *Mook Nayak*, *Vahishkrit Bharat*, and *Equality Janta*, which he started for the protection of *dalit* rights. He also launched numerous movements. One of the memorable struggles of the *Dalits* was the Vaikkom Satyagraha in Travancore in Maharashtra,[5] which asserted the right of the *Dalits* to worship in Hindu temples without hindrance. Another very significant movement was Mahad March[6] to assert the rights of *Dalits* to take water from public watering places. Ambedkar organised the Dalit rally to assert their legal right to take water from the Chowdar tank. The Chowdar tank of Mahad was made a public tank in 1869.

In 1923, the Bombay Legislative Council passed a resolution to the effect that the *Dalits* be allowed to use all public watering places. The Mahad Municipality passed a resolution on 5 January 1927 to the effect that the Municipality had no objection to allowing the Dalits to use the tank. But the higher castes were hesitant in allowing the *Dalits* to use the tank. Soon after this resolution was passed a conference of the *Dalits* of the Colaba district was held for two days. Ambedkar also convened a conference on 18-20 March 1927 on this issue. On 20 March 1927, the conference exhorted the *Dalits* to go to the Chowdar Tank and exercise their right to take water from it. The Hindus who had exhorted them to be bold instantly realised that this was a bombshell and immediately ran away. But the electrified *Dalits* led by Ambedkar marched in a procession through the main streets and for the first time drank the water from Chowdar tank.

Another temple entry movement took place at the Kalaram temple at Nasik in Maharashtra State. On 13 October 1935, at a conference convened on the issue, Ambedkar recounted the experience of the depressed classes and the immense sacrifices made by them to secure minimum human rights under the aegis of Hinduism.[7] Ambedkar fought for the rights of workers and peasants. In the late 1920s and especially in the 1930s when he had formed his Independent Labour Party, he took up the cause of tenants (from both the *dalit* Mahars and the caste Hindu Kunbis) in the Konkan region of Maharashtra. With the support of radicals then in the Congress Socialist Party, the Independent Labour Party organised a huge march of 20,000 peasants to Mumbai in 1938, the largest pre-independence peasant mobilisation in the region. In the same year, Ambedkar joined with the Communists to organise a strike of Mumbai textile workers in protest against a bill about to be introduced by the British Government to curve labour strikes.[8] Ambedkar took the lead in condemning the bill in the assembly and argued that the right to strike was simply another name for the right to freedom of assembly.

British Raj and Protection for *Dalits*

The demand for safeguards and protection of Scheduled Castes (earlier called Depressed Class) has a long history dating to Montague-Chelmsford Reform of 1919 during the British Raj period. Ambedkar had been closely involved in the struggle to give Scheduled Caste people solid statutory safeguard. He was a delegate at the Round Table Conference in London, where he asked for separate electorate for the *Dalits*. It is not a surprise that subsequently Ambedkar saw to it that the welfare of the Scheduled Caste people were guaranteed in the 1949 Constitution of India in the form of reservation in legislative, employment and educational fields. Ambedkar was a great champion of the *dalit* cause because he succeeded in turning the depressed class movement into a revolutionary movement throughout India. Today

India has witnessed the oppressed classes walking on the streets of cities and villages with confidence and poise, of course many despicable acts of discrimination and violence against the *dalits* still occur. Yet the juggernaut of equality is rolling on remorselessly and forcefully.

Conclusion

Ambedkar is India's foremost human rights activist during the twentieth century. He is an emancipator; scholar, extraordinary social reformer and a true champion of human rights.[9] It can be said that he is one of the highly regarded Indians whose emancipation and empowering role for oppressed groups that cut against the gender divide has inspired subaltern groups all over the world. All should try to take inspiration from Dr. B. R. Ambedkar's life and work for the creation of a just and gender-neutral world.

Notes

1. Shyam Lal and K. S. Saxena, editors, *Ambedkar and Nation Building* (Delhi: Rawat Publication, 1998), p. 254.
2. Yogendra Makwana, "Ambedkar- A crusader," in Yogendra Makwana, editor, *Ambedkar and Social Justice* (New Delhi: Publication Division, Government of India), 1992, p. 68.
3. M. S. Gore, *The Social Context of an Ideology* (Delhi: Sage Publication, 1993), pp. 91-97.
4. Vasant Moon, editor, *Dr. Babasaheb Ambedkar Writings and Speeches,* volume 3 (Bombay: Government of Maharashtra, 1987), p. 462, cited in Gail Omvedt, *Ambedkar as a Human Rights Leader*, available in www.ambedkar.org/gail/AmbedkarAs.htm
5. Shyam Lal and K. S. Saxena, *op.cit.*, p. 255.
6. *Babasaheb Ambedkar, Writings and Speeches*, Vol. 5 (Bombay: Government of Maharashtra,1990), pp. 248-252.
7. A K Majunder and Bhanwar Singh, editors, *Ambedkar and Social Justice* (New Delhi: Radha Publications, 1997), pp. 159-165.
8. Gail Omvedt, *op. cit.*
9. Dhananjay Keer, *Ambedkar: Life and Mission* (Bombay: Popular Publication, 1962).

4

Corruption: Violation of Human Rights

Introduction

In common parlance *Corrupt* means 'willing to use power to do dishonest or illegal things in return for money or to get an advantage.' Oxford Dictionary defines 'Corruption' as dishonest or illegal behaviour, especially of people in authority. The purpose of being dishonest is to earn money illegally or influence the work done in ones favour. Similarly, the Webster's Dictionary defines corruption as "inducement to wrong by improper or unlawful means as bribery." Gibbon, a well-known British historian, termed corruption the most infallible symptom in constitutional liberty. Corruption in simple terms can be described as "an act of bribery". It has also been described as "the misuse of public power for private profits in a way that constitutes a breach of law." The most popular and simplest definition of corruption is given by the World Bank. According to this definition corruption is that it is the "abuse of public power for private benefit." Corruption is a very old phenomenon and it can be seen everywhere these days. Corruption is like a cancer in the public life, which has not become overnight, but during the course of time. It has to be rooted out for the progress of any country.

Corruption is wide spread in the society in several forms. No doubt, the people who are having political power, use or misuse or abuse it to earn money illegally or influence to work to be done.

Besides people in power, common man is also involved in corruption in different forms. Forms of corruption vary from people to people. To communicate the intended form of corruption, the corrupt and the corruptible, over the time, have developed a parlance to convey their intension. Thus, the expression like *ooper ki kamaee*, *baksheesh* to the peon in the office, *hafta* to the police constable, and *chaipani* to (*babus*) clerk in the office, *40 percent ki Sarkar* (it became popular during Karnataka election 2023) convey specific meaning, causing no doubt or misgivings. There is no dearth of such expression and no end to the forms of corruption. It takes new forms time to time.

The present chapter is an attempt to study the corruption in India. However, corruption is the violation of Human Rights. This chapter would try to study how corruption is a violation of human rights. This chapter would be confined to corruption in India. Each and every citizen especially women, children have right to development, right to food, right to health etc. This chapter would also study how corruption retards progress and development globally and affects the women, children and minority.

Corruption: A Global Scenario

In countries like India, Pakistan, Indonesia, Bangladesh, Philippines and other third world countries, corruption affects all walks of life. In entire developing regions of Asia, Singapore is the only government that is more or less free from corruption. China has been trying to curb it with an iron hand.

Table 1: The Corruption Index 2022

The perceived levels of public sectors corruption in 180 countries around the world

Rank	SCORE	COUNTRY/ TERRITORY
1	90/100	Denmark
2	87/100	Finland
3	87/100	New Zealand
4	84/100	Norway
5	83/100	Singapore
7	83/100	Switzerland
9	79/100	Germany
19	73/100	Japan

24	69/100	USA
65	45/100	China
85	40/100	India
140	27/100	Pakistan
113	34/100	Nepal
138	28/100	Russia
180	12/100	Somalia

Source: Corruption Perception Index 2022, Transparency International, Berlin, Germany.

The Corruption Perception Index USES A SCALE FROM 0 TO 100. 100 is very clean and 0 is highly corrupt. Despite concerted efforts and many hard-won gains, the Corruption Perception Index of 2022 shows that the scale of corruption is enormous: the global average remains unchanged at a score of 43 out of 100 for the eleventh year running, and more than two-thirds of countries (68 per cent) score below 50. Denmark heads the ranking, with a score of 90. Finland and New Zealand follow closely with a score of 87. Norway, Singapore, Sweden, Switzerland, the Netherlands, Germany, Ireland and Luxembourg complete the top 10 this year, means they are somewhat clean. This year, Somalia, Syria, and South Sudan are at the bottom of the index.

India got 40 score among 180 countries. In 2020 the rank was 86 and 2021 and 2022, it is 85.

Corruption in India

The Corruption rate has been in India and there has been number of cases they can be quoted. One can quote number of cases of corruptions in India, namely, Commonwealth Games scam, 2G, 3G Spectrums, Adarsh Housing, Bafors gun deal, demonetisation, Indian Coal Allocation Scam, Nirav Modi PNB Bank Fraud, Chopper Scam, Satyam Scam, Hawala Scam, Harshad Mehta & Ketan Parekh stock market, Stamp Paper Scam, Bihar Fodder Scam, Sardha Group Financial Scam, Taj Heritage Corridor Case, 46 Corruption Cases against Jayalalita, Madhu Koda Scam (Natural Resources Exploited scam) worth over Rs 4000 crore. There may be more cases and all these cases will not be studied in present chapter. The action is being taken against those involved in various corruption cases. The NCRB has brought out details of corruption cases in various states. Table 2 shows that Maharashtra top the list. It is not only 2019 but also in 2020 as well as 2021.

Table 2: Prevention of Corruption Act & Related Sections of IPC Cases Reported - 2019-2021

	Cases year-wise		
State	**2019**	**2020**	**2021**
Maharashtra	891	664	773
Rajasthan	424	363	501
Tamil Nadu	418	304	423
Karnataka	379	296	360
Odisha	353	245	265
Gujarat	255	199	173
Madhya Pradesh	318	151	250
Punjab	169	143	162
TOTAL ALL INDIA	4244	3100	3745

Source: NCRB 2021, TABLE 8C.1 p. 1

Note: Cases Excluding Cases Registered by CBI as above data is received from States/UTs only.

Corruption: An Issue for Karnataka election for Congress

Beside these scams/corruptions, the Congress party came out with number of corruption cases during Karnataka election in May 2023. During the Karnataka elections May 2023, Cong released 'corruption rate card' and accused BJP of looting over ₹ 15000 crore. Karnataka Congress party leaders alleged that the ruling BJP government in state has "looted" ₹ 1,50,000 crore in the last four years. This was published in daily in English and Kannada. Congress had counted number of examples for these corruption. For example, Congress alleged that "the cost for the CM post is ₹ 2,500 crores while the cost of a ministerial berth is ₹ 500 crore," Congress also mentioned in its 'Corruption rate card'." 40 percent *sarkara* has looted over ₹ 1,50,000 crore from the people of Karnataka in the last 4 years," it alleged. (*Hindustan Time*, May 5, 2023)

The rate card with specific mention about commission, read, "The government demands different deals. It begins with 30 percent commission for the mutt grants, 40 percent for road contracts and goes up to 75 percent for the Covid-19 supplies." In response to this 'corruption rate card,' the Election Commission has issued a notice to the Karnataka Congress over its 'corruption rate card' advertisements published in newspapers targeting the BJP and sought 'empirical' evidence to prove its allegations by Sunday evening. The notice was issued on Saturday following a complaint lodged by the BJP. (*Hindustan Time*, May 6, 2023)

India's money in Swiss Banks have risen for the first time in five years. The quantum of funds held by Indians in Swiss banks had increased in 2006 by about one billion Swiss francs to 6.5 billion Swiss francs (over ₹ 40,000 crore), but fell to less than one-third by end of 2010. In a White Paper on black money tabled in the Parliament in May 2012, the Government had also said that Swiss banks' total liabilities towards Indians have been coming down and fell by more than ₹ 14, 000 crore between 2006 and 2010. The government is trying its best to bring back the unaccounted money from foreign banks including Swiss Bank. BJP Government promised to bring black money to India. Now it is yet arrive India.

Dimensions of corruption

The dimensions of corruption are being changed constantly. Bribe, patronage, nepotism, favouratism, misappropriation, transfers and appointments of officials to lucrative posts, procuring goods or services at rates higher than those prevailing in market with a view to getting commission, forming baseless and unprincipled conditions, trying to get cheap popularity at the cost of State exchequer including installing statutes of their political mentors and forming trust in their names and getting forcible donation of real estate to it, misuse of governmental machinery and illegal occupation of government accommodations etc, are some of the manifest forms of corruption. There can be many more manifestation form of corruption which changes from time to time.

Causes of Corruption

There are number of factors that have been responsible for corruption. The first cause is the emergence of political elite who believe in interest-oriented rather than nation-oriented programmes and policies. After independence in the first two decades the political elites were somewhat honest, dedicated to nation-building. They worked for the country's progress and development. But after two decades, political elites worked only on the basis of some vested interest, namely self-interest, family, caste, region, party and so forth. The planning and programmes were not nation-oriented but they were self-oriented. Even the bureaucrats were concerned with more perks and privileges rather than development-oriented policies for society. Corruption also emerges from power of the government officials of taking decisions like issuing licenses, assessing income tax, giving extensions and so on. Many officials pay thousands and lakhs of rupees to get themselves posted in particular places only because those places enable them to earn thousands and lakh of rupees every month as illegal gratification. This can be considered as causes of corruption.

Secondly, corruption is caused by scarcity. When things required are in short supply, people in power demand consideration to ensure their regular supply or increase their cost. This happens whenever there is high demand but low supply of commodity of daily needs like onion, *Tur dal*, sugar etc. In fact there may not be shortage of goods; it is not properly supplied to people. It is kept in the godown to wait for price-hike. Thirdly, corruption is caused as well as increased because of the change in the value system and ethical qualities of men who administer. Fourthly, corruption can be traced to ineffective administrative organisation. Lack of vigilance, enormous power to the ministerial staff, unaccountability, defective information system, etc., all give scope to officials not only to be corrupt but remain unaffected even after following corrupt practices.

These can be considered as main causes of corruptions anywhere in the world.

1. Lack of Strict and Fast Punishments
2. Lack of Fundamental Rights Awareness among the People
3. Lack of Transparency in Deals and Affairs
4. Lack of Effective Management and Implementation
5. Lack of Economic Stability in India
6. Unhealthy and lack of open Competition and Encouragement in India
7. Low Pay Scales and Wages and *Mahangai*
8. Unemployment (*berojgari*)

Impact of corruption

Corruption also comes when the price is paid but for which no service has been provided. Adulteration in food or spurious drugs sold to patients is corrupt practices seen in our society. Such cases in our daily life are not regarded as corruption because it has become regular phenomenon. In the office it is found that many officials come to office, sign the register and leave office. They become available only when they are offered money for file that they move. No doubt this is corruption. Corruption is found even in most developed countries like the United States of America, Japan, England, France, Canada and Germany. One must not think that corruption is prevalent in India alone. Corruption in its form differs in developed countries. Corruption in developed countries exists only among the highest echelons of business giants, while in India corruption can be seen in every spectrum of our daily life like paying for the railway reservation, for getting admission not only in a professional institution but even for a child in a good primary school, for buying a cinema ticket, for purchasing a gas cylinder, for driving the scooter without a helmet, for getting the arrear-bill passed and so on. All these affect the day-to-day living of the common man and in some way violate human rights. Let us study the effect of corruption in our daily life. (1) It retards economic development of the country in general. (2) It creates violence and lawlessness in society since corrupt man has the money power to influence the executers of law to serve him. (3) It has given rise to casteism and communalism. (4) It affects individuals' character. (5) It develops nepotism. (6) It reduces the credibility of the officials in the eyes of the masses. (7) It increases black money in open market. (8) It creates adulteration of eatables, spurious drugs and shortage of daily needs. (9) It destabilises the government. (10) Rise of Poverty, (11) Power in Wrong hand, etc. Let us study how corruption has some relation to human rights in general and how it becomes a means for human rights violation.

Whole world is concerned about the extent of corruption everywhere. No country is exception to the cancer of corruption. In order to halt the practice of corruption in the world, the world leaders came collectively to put a halt the practice of corruption. All agreed that the corruption is violation of human rights. In the words of former UN Secretary-General Kofi Annan, 'Corruption hurts the poor disproportionately by diverting funds intended for development, undermining a government's ability to provide basic services, feeding inequality and injustice, and discouraging foreign investment and aid.' The UN Convention Against Corruption (UNCAC) came into force on December 14, 2005, and UN's Article 68 (1) has been ratified by 140 countries. Various movements have been launched to bring the attention of government on the issue of corruption. In spite of all these, corruption has touched its height.

Corruption: A Mechanism for Human Rights Violation

There is a close connection between corruption and human rights. Increasing empirical evidence around the world reveals a linkage between corruption and the infringement of human rights. Corrupt state officials use their power to silence critics, so that justice would be subverted. It could be said that corruption causes a lack of respect for human rights and the rule of law.

In India, corruption attacks the fundamental values of human dignity and political equality of the people and hence, there is a pressing need to formulate an act to make a corruption-free society.

Human rights have indeed acquired a special position in the contemporary world because of the increasing tendency of national governments to include these rights in their respective constitution as well as laws. This has resulted in several judiciaries around the world interpreting different human rights as a part of their own national laws or for that matter as a part of the International Law, which their respective country has been a signatory to, through treaties and other conventions. Thus, the Universal Declaration of Human Rights (UDHR), the International Covenant on Civil and Political Rights (ICPR) and the International Covenant on Economic, Social and Cultural Rights (ICESCR) have acquired greater legitimacy in the last few decades as more and more nations have realised the importance of these human rights as instruments for better governance. Probity in governance is an outcome for an efficient system of governance and for socio-economic development. An important requirement for ensuring probity in governance is the absence of corruption. The other requirements may be effective laws, rules and regulations that govern every aspect of public life coupled with effective law enforcement and criminal justice systems.

The right to life, dignity and equality and other important human rights and values depend significantly upon this right. That is, it is a right without which these essential rights lose their meaning. As a fundamental right, the right to a corruption-free society cannot be discarded easily.

Right to Development, Human Rights and Corruption Free-society

The Declaration on the Right to Development, which stated unequivocally that the right to development is a human right, was adopted by the UN in 1986. The Declaration has four main propositions: (1) The right to development is a human right; (2) The human right to development is a right to a particular process of development in which all human rights and fundamental freedoms can be fully realised; (3) The meaning of exercising these rights consistently with freedom implies free, effective, and full participation of all the individuals concerned in decision-making and in the implementation of the process, and therefore, the process must be transparent and accountable, and individuals must have equal opportunity of access to the resources for development and receive a fair distribution of the benefits of development, (4) The right confers an unequivocal obligation on duty-holders, individuals within the community, states at the national level, and states at the international level. Nation-states have the responsibility to help realise the process of development by initiating appropriate development policies. International agencies have the obligation to cooperate with the nation-states to facilitate the realisation of the process of development. It is in this context that the fundamental right to a corruption-free society adds a new and necessary dimension to the right to development. No development process will have any meaning and relevance if corruption as an institutionalised process interferes with people's struggles to realise their right to development. Corruption retards the right to development.

Human Rights and Corruption: An Inter-relationship

If corruption is shown to violate human rights, this will influence public attitudes. Identifying the specific links between corruption and human rights may persuade key actors – public officials, parliamentarians, judges, prosecutors, lawyers, business people, bankers, accountants, the media and the public in general – to take a stronger stand against corruption. This may be so even in countries where reference to human rights is sensitive. Connecting acts of corruption to violations of human rights also creates new possibilities for action, especially if, as we will argue, acts of corruption can be challenged using the different national, regional and international mechanisms that exist to monitor compliance with human rights. In the last seventy eight years, the Universal Declaration of Human Rights (UDHR) and many more mechanisms have been created to hold states and individuals accountable for human rights violations. When acts of corruption are linked to violations of human rights, all these institutions could act to force accountability and so create disincentives for corruption.

Vulnerability and disadvantage

While corruption violates the rights of all those affected by it, it has a disproportionate impact on people that belong to groups such as minorities, indigenous peoples, migrant workers, disabled people that are exposed to particular risks. It also disproportionately affects women and children. Corruption in such cases can magnify and intensify human rights problems of such groups. Many migrant workers during the Covid-19, had to suffer a lot. They could not get services/help from government and had to travel to their houses on bi-cycle with old parents.

Corruption and violation of Women Rights

Corruption impacts men and women differently and reinforces and perpetuates existing gender inequalities. Women's lack of access to political and economic power excludes them from networks that permit access to decision-making bodies. Where institutions are controlled by men, women do not have enough power to challenge corruption. Women's access to justice is compromised in other ways. Many women also have fewer opportunities than men to acquire higher education, or obtain land, credit and other productive assets. When they have access to work, they are often paid lower salaries. They tend to assume the domestic responsibilities of taking care of children and older adults, which means they are financially dependent, cannot work or are poorer. For all these reasons – but essentially because women are over-represented in the poorest social segments of society and under-represented in decision-making bodies – corruption affect them in particular ways, often disproportionately.

Corruption and Children's Rights

Corruption may also have a disproportionate impact on children. While children possess in general the same civil, political, economic, social and cultural rights as adults, they also have certain rights specific to them. Most of these are identified in the 1989 United Nations Convention on the Rights of the Child (CRC), in Article 24 of the International Covenant on Civil and Political Rights (ICCPR), and in Article 10(3) of the International Covenant on Economic, Social and Cultural Rights (ICESCR). Corruption can violate many of the rights that children share with adults, including the right to life and the right to health. In addition, some rights, such as the right to education, are particularly important to children. Corruption in the education sector very often violates the rights of children. In India, Constitution guaranty the Right to Education. Children are given free meal in schools. There have been scams on Mid-day meal. This is a sheer violation of Child Right.

Corruption, Poverty and Human Rights

Corruption has a severely detrimental impact on the lives of people living in poverty when compared with higher income groups. Corruption not only affects economic growth and discourages foreign investment, thereby indirectly affecting the poor, but reduces the net income of those living in poverty, distorts policies, programmes and strategies that aim to meet their basic needs, and diverts public resources from investments in infrastructure that are crucial elements of strategies to lift them out of poverty. Whenever corruption is generalised, poor people are as exposed as others to the small-scale bribery of public officials (notably in the healthcare, law enforcement and judicial sectors) but the effect on their purse will be heavier. Large-scale corruption, meanwhile, damages the quality of public services on which the poor depend particularly, to meet basic needs. Hence, corruption breeds poverty and infringes human rights globally.

Corruption, Indigenous People and Minorities and Human Rights

Indigenous people and minorities suffer particularly from corruption. They are often among the poorest and most disadvantaged groups in society. Indigenous women are additionally exposed to risk. Indigenous communities that are closely linked to land they live on collectively are especially vulnerable to corruption of infrastructure programmes that displace them, and smaller-scale corruption associated with land sales and registration. Many indigenous communities also lack access to education and are consequently less aware of their legal rights. Mechanisms for reporting and tackling corruption are often out of their reach. Since indigenous voices are rarely heard in policy discussions, these populations often have little influence on the design and implementation of anti-corruption policies and programmes that could improve their status. Today farmers are facing a lot of problems due to the land scams everywhere. Corruption, land scam takes away the rights of farmers to cultivate.

Corruption Violates Socio-economic and Cultural Rights

Corruption is likely to violate enjoyment of cultural rights. States have a wide range of duties to provide or regulate public services in relation to health, housing, water and education. These services generate large public contracts which not only create opportunities for corruption but have a disproportionate impact on vulnerable and disadvantaged groups, in particular women. Widespread corruption in health or educational services deters the poor from seeking healthcare and education and depresses living standards and opportunities for poorer people in particular. Corruption will have an impact on the enjoyment of all economic, social and cultural rights.

Corruption and Right to Food

The right to food also referred to as the right of everyone to be free from hunger, is a component of the more general right to an adequate standard of living (ICESCR, Article 11(2)). The right to adequate food asserts that all people should be in a position to feed themselves. It should be made clear that the right to food does not imply that states must provide food to everyone. The obligation on a state is to take steps that will gradually make it possible for all people to feed themselves, will provide access to food in an equal and non-discriminatory way, and will assist people to obtain food if they are not in a position to feed themselves. Sometime we find the food-grains which are to be sold in Public Distribution Scheme are being sold on higher price. Price hike of food-grain in some way is due to corruption and that violates right to food of poor mass. Now the BJP Government at Centre has started providing 5 kg free grains to 80 crore people in all States.

Corruption may also affect other elements of the right to food. Food security may be compromised if food producers obtain licenses by bribing the authorities; and the right to health (and life) may be compromised, if such food producers subsequently put adulterated or unsafe products on the market. Corruption in food programmes and schemes designed to meet the needs of socially vulnerable people may also prevent them from obtaining food; when a person embezzles funds from a food programme, or diverts food into the black market for personal profit, the right to food of those who are embezzled is clearly compromised.

Corruption violates the right to adequate housing

The right to adequate housing derives from the right to an adequate standard of living. It focuses on the obligation to ensure that everyone has housing that is safe, healthy and adequate (ICESCR, Article 11(1)). In addition, the right forbids discrimination in the field of housing, as well as forced or arbitrary evictions or acts of unjust dispossession. The right to adequate housing does not entail that the government has to build housing for the entire population or that housing must be provided free of charge to whoever requests it. It is primarily a right of access. What constitutes adequate is dependent on social, economic, climatic, ecological and other factors. However, certain minimum elements are integral to the right and should always be taken into account. Corruption may violate this right by restricting one or more of its elements. The *Adarsh* apartment scam in Mumbai is the glaring example before us. Those who were supposed get their houses are living in *juggi-jhopadi*. Now *Pradhan Mantri Awash Yojna* has been proving house to poor people.

Corruption and Health

Corrupt practices in the pharmaceutical industry are prevalent everywhere. Unethical drug promotion can generate conflicts of interest for physicians and ultimately can harm patients' health. If drug marketing by pharmaceutical companies is not well regulated, it may not benefit to patients. If states do not guard against this kind of abuse, they will violate their duty to protect the right to health. In general terms, corruption in the health sector, occurs in three main forms: in management of financial resources (budget allocation, etc.); in the distribution of medical supplies (purchasing, marketing); and in the relationships of health workers with patients. Now Generic medicine is being promoted by government. This helps the poor people to get medicine on reasonable rate.

Conclusion

Human rights and corruption are related in ways in which corruption leads to violations of human rights. Acts of corruption can directly and indirectly violate human rights, especially those of the disadvantaged. Anti-corruption measures need a human rights perspective. Similarly, effective human rights protection measures need to incorporate and integrate anti-corruption measures as well.

When violations of human rights are portrayed as a result of corruption, it will raise the awareness of people concerning the consequences of corruption on the well-being of individuals. This perspective helps to demonstrate clearly to the public the destructive effects of corruption on human beings. Trafficking in human beings is so inhumane that it might create a common spirit and public support for the cause of attempting to limit or eliminate corruption. The negative impacts of corruption on humanity would thus be more convincing and tangible to the public. People will have more understanding about the detrimental effects of corruption when they see that it can threaten their lives. They will have greater sympathy for the victims of corruption because they are the same victims of human rights violations. Any individual could become one of the unfortunate victims if the state is not able to protect them and if the public remains passive and unaware. Public support for combating corruption will create demands and put pressure on the government to be committed more seriously to this cause and generate the true political will to eradicate corruption. Giving a human face to corruption may lead to more effective anti-corruption strategies through better awareness of the destructive effects of corruption, which should no longer be tolerated. People should be told about the relevant of the Prevention of Corruption Act (PCA), 1988. Prevention of Money Laundering Act, 2002 is to be applied seriously. Each State must have *Lokayukta* as per *Lokpal* and *Lokayukta* Act 2013.

Considering the issues of corruption and human rights through the lens of power relations enables us to see them as relationship between different social groups or individuals who are able to access power differently. Let's launch a mass movement to combat corruption from this universe.

References

Choudhry, P. C., "Corruption" in *Seminar* No. 421, September, 1994.

Ahuja Ram, Social Problems in India, Rawat Publication, Jaipur, 1997, and 2003, pp. 449-474.

Anukansai, Kanokkan., "Corruption: The Catalyst for violation of Human Rights, *BACC Journal,* July 2010, pp. 6-15.

Corruption and Human Rights: Integrating Human Rights into the anti-corruption Agenda: Challenges, possibilities and opportunities. Draft Report February 2009, International Council on Policy, Human Rights, Switzerland.

Santhanam Committee Report on "Prevention of Corruption", Government of India, 1964.

The Impact of Corruption on the Human Rights based Approach to Development, United Nations Development Programme Oslo Governance Centre 2004, *Hindustan Times*, May 5, 2023.

5

Violence Against Women

Introduction

The use of physical force or brute power for achieving one's ends is called violence. It is an innate instinct witnessed in all living creatures, be they human or animal. Violence may be the consequence of anger or an individual's reaction of self-defence in what one perceives to be a threatening situation. Human history is replete with instances of perpetual conflict that are manifested in violence. As Karl Marx said, "*The history of all hitherto existing society is the history of class struggle.*" The context of Marx's statement is the revolt of the proletarians or members of the working class against the bourgeoisie or capitalists in retaliation for their exploitation by the latter. Convinced that violence could be the means to eliminate the power of the bourgeoisie, Marx coined the slogan, "*Workers of the world, unite, you have nothing to lose but the chains of slavery,*" thereby inciting the workers to perpetrate violence against the ruling capitalist class, though with a decisive outcome in mind.

Violence is actually a complex problem, arising out of various psychological, cultural, political and religious factors. By its very nature, it is a destructive force and needs to be curbed at the very outset. The problem of violence has assumed alarming proportions in the contemporary era, which is characterised by rapidly escalating violence and terror, which have infested virtually all sections of society, and impacted virtually every nation in the world. In this an attempt is made to study one aspect of violence affecting Indian society, viz. the various forms of violence being unleashed against women. Crime against women can be seen as cruelty by husband and relatives, Molestation, Kidnapping and Abduction of Women, Rape, Sexual Harassment, Dowry Death and Attempt to Rape. This study is preceded by an analysis of the concept of violence. The study is based on Crime in India report 2021. An attempt is also made to analyse the concept of violence.

Praxis of Violence

It can be observed that the use of force is an intrinsic part of any act of violence, be it physical or psychological. Coercion is the use of either physical or intangible force to compel action that is contrary to the will or reasoned judgment of the individual or group subjected to such force. We can, therefore, say that violence is the wilful application of such a force in way that it physically or psychologically injures or causes damage to the person, group or property against whom it is applied. Actually, a study of the dynamics of violence has long been a preoccupation of social scientists of all ideological persuasions.

The term 'violence' is also associated with several meanings, as can be observed in the rapidly growing literature on the subject. The dictionary meaning of 'violence' is the exercise of physical force so as to inflict injury or damage to any person(s) or property. This infliction of injury or damage could be both spiritual and non-spiritual. In both the senses, however, violence leads to destructiveness, and symbolises an act perpetrated by one person against the freedom of another. Margaret has defined violence as 'the unsanctioned damage to a person or property'.[1] On the other hand, Han'nah Arendt, contends that violence in itself is neither beastly nor irrational, and that all violence as such is not condemnable. Some theorists have also distinguished between 'good violence' and 'bad violence'. But violence by itself is neither good nor bad; it is the way in which it is used that makes it good or bad. In fact, violence is harmful only if it takes the form of an unsanctioned damage to any person(s) or property. Violence can also be perceived as man's struggle to adapt to his environment.[2]

According to the Random House Dictionary of English Language, "*violence means rough or injurious physical force, action or treatment*". In other words, it is the expression of an individual's aggressive drive on both the personal and social levels. Personal violence is a violent act of a man or woman against another man or woman -such as assault and rape, homicide. Social violence, on the other hand, is manifested in actions and situations like genocide, the concentration camps set up by the Nazi regime in Germany to exterminate Jews during the Second World War, and communal riots. Some scholars have tried to relate violence with aggression. However, Daniels has a different view in this regard. He points out that 'aggression' represents an entire spectrum of assertive, intrusive and attacking behaviour. Violence, as a specialised sub-form of aggression, is accompanied by a strong, uncontrollable emotion like anger or hostility; and anger occurs when a plan of action towards a valued goal is interrupted by something specific enough to warrant attack[3] or "when the expected rewards for attack override other outcomes".[4] According to the Encyclopedia of Social Sciences,[5] in the social context, violence may be roughly defined as the illegal employment of methods of physical coercion for achieving personal or group ends. It is distinct from force or power, which is a purely physical concept.

The genesis of violence in ancient society can be traced back to the times of Abel and Cain, as mentioned in the *Old Testament* Bible of the Christians and Jews. As has been mentioned above, violence can be considered as a form of unsanctioned damage to any person or property. In ancient societies, man would glory in the use of violence and the man of war would be considered a hero. It is no wonder then that violence also has a scriptural sanction. Since scriptures are ancient books of authority, many primordial instincts and customs find a justification in some of these sacred books. Even today, the practice of sacrificing children to god for some wish fulfilment in return is prevalent in Indian society. There are also instances of human beings having been sacrificed to please the god of rain and engender bountiful rainfall in return.[6] The history of the world thus shows that violence is a universal phenomenon. Even more paradoxical is the close relationship between violence and human progress as has been seen through the side effects of war. Ironically, advancements in science and technology have not been able to achieve any reduction in violence but have, in fact, provided more effective and more reliable instruments of perpetrating torture and violence on humans. Developments in science are indeed directly proportional to developments in various forms of violence. Today we have the nuclear bomb, which is a potential threat to all of humanity in the entire universe. More and more weapons continue to be manufactured to unleash waves of violence and to destroy humanity in all corners of the globe.[7]

This unabated rise in the manufacture of tools of violence and its perpetration against all forms of life is the biggest danger to our society and our culture. These weapons of war and destruction are poisoning our most precious institutions, among them schools and universities, and annihilating the spirit of trust and co-operation that is fundamental for their efficient functioning. As the noted socialist Madhu Dandavate avers, violence has always been the manifestation of some form of frustration in society and is expressed through physical force. These frustrations are further engendered through social maladies, including caste and class-related tensions, and also the rise of unemployment among educated youth, who fail to find a suitable outlet for their aspirations, and therefore react through physical and verbal violence.

In this chapter an effort is being made to study three critical forms of violence against women, namely, violence in the form of rape, domestic violence, and dowry deaths.

In general, crime rate in India has been increasing. The crime rate consist of all types of crime in India. This also includes different head-wise crime against women in India. Out of 36,63,360 crimes in India, 4,28,278 crimes are committed against women India as per 2021 NCRB. It means 11.69 percent crime is committed against women in India. This chapter will focus on different types of crimes committed against women in India.

Table 1: Crime Rate in India (all types of crimes)
At a glance - IPC Crimes over the years 2012 – 2021

Year	Registered cases	Crime Rate
2012	2387188	196.7
2013	2647722	215.5
2014	2851563	229.2

2015	2949400	234.2
2016	2975711	233.6
2017	3062579	237.7
2018	3132955	236.7
2019	3225597	241.2
2020	4254356	314.3
2021	3663360	268.0

Source: Crime in India 2021 (NCRB) p. x.

Crime Against Women

There have been a number of violent crimes constantly committed against women. The Ministry of Home Affairs (Government of India) has brought out a comprehensive report (NCRB, 2021) regarding the different types of crimes that women in India are subjected to. This report reveals shocking data about these violent crimes against women. Women continue to be ill-treated, raped and killed on the issue of dowry, despite the passage of the Domestic Violence against Women Act in 2005. Crimes against women include cases of rape, outraging modesty, dowry deaths, harassment, acid attacks, and kidnappings.

Table 2: Crime against women 2021

	Type of Crime	Total
1.	Cruelty by husband and relatives	137956
2.	Molestation	414
3.	Kidnapping and abduction of women	76263
4.	Rape	31677
5.	Sexual Harassment	3811
6.	Dowry Death	6795
7.	Attempt to Rape	3811
	Total crime committed against women	428278

Source: NCRB 2021, (Ministry of Home Affairs, Government of India,)

Over 4,28,278 lakh cases of crimes against women were registered during 2021, which means there is an increase of 15.3 percent over 2020 (3,71,503 lakh) and in 2019 at 4,05,326. The 2021 report also shows that like 2020 data, cases of assault on women with the intent to outrage her modesty formed the next big category of crime against women at 20.8 percent in 2021 followed by kidnapping and abduction (17.6 percent) and rape (7.4 percent). Among states and Union territories, Uttar Pradesh saw the highest number of such cases, with 56,083, followed by Rajasthan (40,738), Maharashtra (39,526), West Bengal (35884), Madhya Pradesh (30,673) and Delhi 14,277 as per 2021 NCRB data. However, in terms of rate of crime against women in 2021, Uttar Pradesh (50.0), Rajasthan (105.4), Maharashtra (66.0), West Bengal (74.6). Among the top listed states were Assam (168.3) followed by Delhi (147), Odisha (137), and Haryana (119.7) and Telangana (111.2). In 2021, the crime rate registered per lakh women population was at 64.5 that is much higher in comparison with 56.5 in 2020. The crime rate was 62.3 in 2019 and 58.8 in 2018.

The overall cases of crime against women reflected a slight decline of 8.3 percent from over 4.05 lakh cases in 2019 to around 3.71 lakh cases in 2020, the year when the Covid-19 pandemic hit the world resulting in repeated lockdowns in India. Crime against women under Indian Panel Code (IPC) in 2021 were registered under 'cruelty by husband or relatives' accounting for 31.8 percent or 1.36 lakh cases. The percentage was nearly 2 percent higher than 2020.

Table 3: Crime against Women (IPC+SLL) - 2018-2021

State	2018	2019	2020	Rate of Total Crime against Women (2020)	Crime Against women 2021
Uttar Pradesh	59445	59853	49385	45.1	56083
West Bengal	30394	29859	36439	76.2	35884
Rajasthan	27866	41550	34535	90.5	40738
Maharashtra	35497	37144	31954	53.8	39526
Assam	27687	30025	26352	154.3	29046
Madhya Pradesh	28942	27560	25640	63.3	30673
All India TOTAL STATE(S)	360339	387997	357363	55.9	428278
Delhi	13640	13395	10093	106.4	

Source: NCRB, TABLE 3A.1 Page 1 of 1.

Rape as violence

India registered 31,677 cases of rape in 2021 - an average 86 daily - while nearly 49 cases of crime against women were lodged every single hour, according to the latest government report on crimes in the country. Rape cases accounted for 7.5 percent of total cases in 2020 and 7.9 percent in 2019. In terms of numbers, in 2021 there were 31,677 cases of rape involving 31,878 victims. As many as 3,038 victims were below 18 and of them 183 were between 6 to 12 years and 53 girls were less than six years old. The report in a separate section lists cases of murder with rape and gangrape and puts the number of incidents at 284 involving 293 victims in 2021. The number of rape cases in 2020 was 28,046, while it was 32,033 in 2019. Among states, Rajasthan (6,337) was on top of the list followed by Madhya Pradesh (2,947), Maharashtra (2,496) and Uttar Pradesh (2,845), while Delhi recorded 1,250 rape cases in 2021.

Table 4: Total number Rape Cases in India in 2021

S. No.	State	Cases
1.	Rajasthan	6337
2.	Madhya Pradesh	2947
3.	Uttar Pradesh	2845
4.	Maharashtra	2496
5.	Assam	1733
6.	Haryana	1716
7.	Odisha	1456
8.	Jharkhand	1425
9.	Delhi	1250
10.	Andhra Pradesh	1184
11.	West Bengal	1123

Source: NCRB, 2021.

If we study the NCRB report 2021, one finds that out of total rape cases in India (31,677) Child rape was 3033. That means 9.57 percent cases are reported as child rape cases. There may be more than that, but many cases are un-reported. There can be the cases of very minor child rape that must have gone un-reported as parents may not like to report to police.

Table 5: Child (below 18 year old) Rape in India in 2021

S. No.	State	Cases
1.	Rajasthan	1452
2.	Andhra Pradesh	614
3.	Jharkhand	295
4.	Uttar Pradesh	256
5.	Himachal Pradesh	215

Source: NCRB, 2021 Table 3A.2 (i) p. 218.

Children are among the most vulnerable victims of sexual abuse because society treats them as non-entities. In Indian society, children are brought up and conditioned to believe that adults know best and that the latter are never wrong. Consequently, the child never learns to say 'no' to an adult and is often docile in front of them. Many adults take undue advantage of this situation and exploit children sexually. In spite of having introduced POSCO Act 2012 (updated on 29/02/2023) child rape continues in India. This table reveals that Rajasthan (1452) top the list of Child rape in India. What is POSCO Act 2012? The Protection of Children from sexual Offences Acts 2012 (ACT NO. 32 OF 2012 [19th June, 2012.]) is an Act to protect children from offences of sexual assault, sexual harassment and pornography and provide for establishment of Special Courts for trial of such offences and for matters connected therewith or incidental thereto.

Crimes against children increased in India by 16.2 percent between 2020 and 2021, according to the latest National Crime Records Bureau (NCRB) data. There were just under 1.5 lakh cases of crimes against children registered in 2020 across all states and Union Territories. This includes child sexual abuse, abduction, murder, child marriage among other crimes. The total crime rate went up from 28.9 percent in 2020 to 33.6 percent in 2021. The crime rate is the number of incidences of crime registered per lakh population.[8]

The NCRB, 2021 reveals that there were 65,025 rape cases reported and the sad part is that the accused were known to the victims in 96.8 percent. Among all Indian States Rajasthan was recorded the highest number of rape cases (6337), followed by Madhya Pradesh (2947) and Uttar Pradesh (2845). Rajasthan reported the highest number of rape cases in the country in 2021, with an increase of more than 19 percent in comparison to 2020. This report also reveals that among in five states, namely, Maharashtra Manipur, Nagaland and Sikkim where 100 percent of victims knew their rapists before. The maximum number of rape cases in India were committed by "family, friends, neighbours or other known persons". As many as 3,038 victims were below 18 and of them 183 were between 6 to 12 years and 53 girls were less than six years old.

Table 6: Offenders Relation to Victims of Rape (Section 376 IPC) - 2021

State	Cases Offender known to Victim (Total)	Family Members	Friends/ Online Friends or Live in Partners on Pretext of Marriage / Separated Husband	Family Friends/ Neighbours/ Employer or Other Known Persons	Cases Offenders Unknown or Not Identified	Total rape case (known+ unknown offender)	Percentage Share of Known Cases to Total Rape Cases
Rajasthan	6074	582	1701	3791	263	6337	95.8
Madhya Pradesh	2898	292	1145	1461	49	2947	98.3
Uttar Pradesh	2668	149	1123	1396	177	2845	93.8
Maharashtra	2496	163	1425	908	0	2496	100
Assam	1709	177	482	1050	24	1733	98.6
Haryana	1697	128	523	1046	19	1716	98.9
Odisha	1455	2	2133	220	1	1456	99.9

Source: NCRB, 2021, TABLE 3A.4 Page 1 of 1.

Out of 31,677 cases of rape, 28,147 or 89% of rape cases were committed either by friends (including online friends), live-in partners (on the pretext of marriage), separated husbands or family friends, employers or other known person. India registered 31,677 cases of rape in 2021 - an average 86 daily - while nearly 49 cases of crime against women were lodged every single hour, according to the latest government report on crimes in the country.

Among the rape victims are not only girls belonging to poor families but also office-going women usually belonging to the middle class, who are often sexually harassed by their employers. Women are, in fact molested, humiliated and raped in almost setting ranging from the jail to hospital to workplaces. Incidents of rape are, in fact, rising alarmingly in India.

As per data available from the 2021 report of the National Crime Records Bureau, 1,23,407 children were kidnapped or abducted during the year 2020-2021 in various states and Union Territories in India. There are states recorded the highest number of cases of kidnapping of children in the country, viz. –Uttar Pradesh 3515, Bihar 2923, Punjab 1372 and Madhya Pradesh. Around 53276 children were reported to have been sexually assaulted, during 2020-2021. As per the data for the year 2020-2021, the states of Uttar Pradesh, Maharashtra and Madhya Pradesh recorded, 7001, 6219, and 6027 cases of sexual assault, respectively during the year 2020-2021.

Dowry Death and Domestic Violence

Incidents of dowry death and domestic violence are also very common in north India. The prevalence of dowry is, in fact, like a plague spreading across most Indian cities, with an increasing number of urban, educated, middle class women falling prey to it. In fact, there are reports of dowry deaths virtually every day in the media, as the discovery of the charred body of any woman, particularly a young bride, is usually perceived as a dowry death, which may be a case of suicide caused by harassment by the husband and/or in-laws of the woman, or murder of the woman by her spouse and/or his family. There may not be increase in dowry death but it continues in India. Uttar Pradesh tops in dowry death as per 2021 NCRB. Second in the row come Bihar where it 1000 dowry death cases were reported.

Table 7: Dowry Death 2021

Sl. No.	State	Cases
1.	Uttar Pradesh	2235
2.	Bihar	1000
3.	Madhya Pradesh	523
4.	Rajasthan	454
5.	West Bengal	454

Source: NCRB, 2021Table 3A.2 (i) p. 212.

A bill on domestic violence, called the Protection of Women from Domestic Violence Act (PWDVA), was passed in Parliament in 2005 and came into effect in 2006. The much-welcomed Act aims to provide protection and compensation to women for all kinds of abuse at home, including physical, sexual, verbal, emotional and economic abuse. The new law requires a sentence to be passed within 90 days of the first hearing. However, in many states, the implementation of this Act has been abysmally poor. There is a provision for the appointment of Protection Officers in some states, who are authorised to help the women victims in attaining justice within the earliest possible time. Sometime one notices that the Protection Officers are, however, over-burdened with work and are thus reluctant to take on additional responsibilities.

These figures are largely indicative, as dowry deaths have continued to occur in the country even after the advent of the PWDVA. The PWDVA came into effect when in the wake of public protests against these deaths, it was finally accepted that both nationally as well as internationally, women in India were being subjected to a form of culture-specific violence termed as 'dowry violence'. This often culminated in the woman's death, or a 'dowry death'. Such deaths also often provided the husband and his family a convenient means of getting rid of an 'unwanted' bride and seeking another, who would bring more dowry than her predecessor. However, while this practice eventually led to the enactment of the PWDVA, the implementation of this Act is not easy, as unfortunately, Indian society is not divided into two clear and mutually exclusive categories of dowry takers and dowry givers. This is because in most cases, the boy's parents or dowry takers also happen to be dowry givers when they marry off their daughters. It is this unique social ethos that prevents the effective implementation of the PWDVA and therefore a reduction in the incidence of dowry violence in India.

Table 8: Dowry Death (Decadal Differences)

S. No.	Year	Cases	Rise/Decline in Dowry death (Percent)
1.	2013	8083	-----
2.	2014	8455	+4.60%
3.	2015	7634	-10.75
4.	2016	7621	-0.17%
5.	2017	7466	-2.07%
6.	2018	7167	-4.17%
7.	2019	7141	-0.36%
8.	2020	6966	-2.51%
9	2021	6753	-3.15%

Source: According to data shared by Union Ministry of State for Home, Ajay Kumar Mishra in Rajya Sabha on December 14, 2022.

Table depicts that there is a decline in the dowry death in India. There may be various reason for the decline of dowry death. It may be because nowadays love-marriages are encouraged. Young people believe in looking for their own partners and the matter of dowry does not come in picture. Second reason may be the inter-caste marriage. In certain caste system, there may not be the provision for dowry system. Third reason may be that young generation are aware of PWDVA Act. They know the consequence of dowry system. These are the main reasons for the decline of dowry death.

Conclusion

It has been observed that incidents of domestic violence against women and dowry deaths continue to exist in Indian society despite many legislations and the enactment of the Protection of Women from Domestic Violence Act (PWDVA), POSCO 2012 and etc. In fact, crimes against women have shown an increasing trend over the years. Violence against women is thus akin to a parasite, which has a vice-like grip over the body politic of the entire country. Many social activists and reformers have tried their best to combat this scourge of violence and attempted to introduce schemes for the upliftment of women, particularly those belonging to the marginalised sections. Obviously the spread of education is one of the potent antidotes to this menace. The empowerment and enfranchisement of women are the keys for achieving an end to the mistreatment of women in any form. It is thus imperative to mobilise social forces and the intellectual capital of the entire society in the country in order to bring the perpetrators of violence to justice. Social activists can come forward to help government to combat such type of violence against women. Especially women groups should come forward to eschew crime against women. Number of human rights activists working in India should identify the victims and try to help those victims. The path towards the achievement of this goal is full of hurdles but that should not deter us from battling the odds and ushering in a just and equitable society that treats its women with respect and dignity.

Notes

1. Kumar, Mahendra (1975). *Violence and Non-violence in International Relations*, Thomson Press, India, p. 46.
2. *Ibid,* p. 47.
3. Daniels, D.N., *et al.* (1970). *Violence and the Struggle for Existence*, Little Brown and Company, Boston, p. 98.
4. *Ibid,* p. 14.
5. Hook, Sidney (ed.) (1935). *Violence, In Encyclopaedia of the Social Sciences,* Vol. 15, Macmillan Company, New York., p. 264.
6. Gupta, Narendra Nath (1945). "Side Lights on the National Movement in India", Vol. I, *Gandhi and Gandhism*, Kitabs, Bombay, p. 194.
7. Aiyar, S.P. (1967). "Anatomy of Mass Violence", in S.P. Aiyar (ed.) *The Politics of Mass Violence in India*, Manaktala and Sons, Bombay, pp. 29–30.
8. https://www.thenewsminute.com/article/crimes-against-children-increases-162-child-sexual-abuse-cases.

References

Aiyar, S.P. (1967). "Anatomy of Mass Violence", in S.P. Aiyar (ed.) *The Politics of Mass Violence in India*, Manaktala and Sons, Bombay, pp. 29–30.

Daniels, David N., Marshall F. Gilula, Frank M. O (1970). *Violence and the Struggle for Existence*, Little, Brown and Company, Boston.

Government of India (GoI) (2021). *Crime in India,* Ministry of Home Affairs, New Delhi.

Gupta, Narendra Nath (1945). "Side Lights on the National Movement in India", Vol. I, *Gandhi and Gandhism*, Kitabs, Bombay, p. 194.

Hook, Sidney (ed.) (1935). *Violence, In Encyclopaedia of the Social Sciences,* Vol. 15, Macmillan Company, New York.

Kumar, Mahendra (1975). *Violence and Non-violence in International Relations*, Thomson Press, India.

6

Democracy and Human Rights: A Dialectical Relationship

Introduction

Almost all societies have developed certain rights that have to be respected, protected and followed. In 1948, all nations came together and adopted and proclaimed the Universal Declaration of Human Rights. All these rights have been listed in the UN Declaration of Human Rights of 1948. No matter how great a nation may be, yet it has to abide and conform to Human Rights Laws. It is because all nations agreed the Charter and signed. Today most of countries of twenty-first century have adopted democratic system of government. At the same time there are countries, not been practicing democratic pattern of government even though they are the signatory of the UN Declaration of Human Rights of 1948. Are they able to protect the Human Rights of their citizens in their countries? The present study is an attempt to study how non-democratic countries are able to protect Human Right of their citizens. The study will try to find out whether there is any relationship between Democracy and Human Rights at all. The study will find out the true relationships between two concepts, viz., democracy and Human Rights.

Defining Democracy

People generally consider the term 'democracy' a western

concept. It is derived from the Greek word, '*demos*' which means the people; and '*kratia*' stands for rule or government. Abraham Lincoln gave a very popular definition which is known even by the school going children. It reads: '*democracy is the government of the people, by the people, and for the people.*' In short, "democracy as a form of government implies that the ultimate authority of governance in this system is vested in the ordinary people so that public policy is made to conform to the will of the people and to serve the interests of the people."[1] If it is a rule for the people and by the people, then the democratic government must serve its citizens. But then again, democracy is no longer equated with the mere ability to hold regular elections as it has been happening in the developing countries. This is just the starting point of development of society. It has become mandatory to hold free and fair election periodically by each and every nation. Democracy does not mean only to hold regular election but to protect the basic rights of its citizens.

No doubt, democracy has three basic guiding principles, namely, liberty, equality and fraternity. French revolution was fought on these three principles. Since it is peoples' government, it must protect the rights of its citizens. The government is accountable / responsible to people who have put them in power. Question arises what will happen when there is dictatorial government who have also signed the Universal Declaration of Human Rights in 1948. All signatory countries will have to protect the rights of people in their countries.

The values of freedom, respect for human rights and the principle of holding periodic free and fair elections by universal suffrage are considered to be essential elements of democracy. Hence, democracy must nurture the natural environment for the protection and effective realisation of human rights in any country. That would be the true meaning of democracy. All these values are embodied / enshrined in the Universal Declaration of Human Rights and further developed in the International Covenant on Civil and Political Rights. Maximum countries of the world have developed their democratic ideals based on these principles. The framer of our Indian Constitution has been guided by these principles and some of the chapters were borrowed from these guidelines.

Defining Human Rights

Whenever one thinks of Human Rights, one is reminded of the *UN Declaration of Human Rights* of 1948. On December 10, 1948, the General Assembly of the United Nations adopted and proclaimed the Universal Declaration of Human Rights. Human Rights are generally defined as the rights which every human being is entitled to enjoy. Each and every human being has to enjoy certain rights as being human. "Human rights are those rights that belong to everyone as a member of the human race, regardless of skin colour, nationality, political convictions or religious persuasion, social standing, gender or age. Every individual possesses human rights. They are subjective rights because the right-holders of human rights are individuals, and not collective. Human rights are rights with a certain complexity because they are at the same time moral, legal, and political rights."[2]

That is why almost all societies have developed certain rights that have to be respected and followed. In 1948, all the members of the UNO (that time there were 51 countries and today there are 193 countries who are signatory to this declaration) came together and adopted and proclaimed the universal declaration of Human Rights. All these rights have been listed in the ***UN Declaration of Human Rights*** of 1948. "No matter how great a nation may be yet it has to abide and conform to Human Rights Laws. It is because all nations agreed the Charter and signed. Human Rights Laws do have some primacy over the laws of various nations."[3]

Most of countries of twenty-first century have adopted democratic system of government. Though they adopted the ***UN Declaration of Human Rights* of 1948** and became signatory of the same, still, there are many countries not been practicing democratic pattern of government. But then the question arises, how they are able to protect the Rights of their citizens in their countries? The present study is an attempt to study how non-democratic countries are able to protect/safeguard Human Rights. The present study will try to find out whether there is any relationship between Democracy and Human Rights at all. The study will find out the complex relationship between two concepts, viz., Democracy and Human Rights.

Democracy without Protection of Human Rights and Pro-Poor Development Programmes is a Myth

All democratic countries must put all effort to alleviate poverty, as it is considered as the brutal denial of human rights. "Poverty is a situation that gives rise to a feeling of acute discrimination, as what one has and what one should have".[4] Again, right to life is a fundamental right, enshrine in Article 21 of our Indian constitution. This must be recognised at the outset by all policy-makers, including governments, donor agencies, international organisations and non-governmental organisation (NGOs). Poverty is a condition generated by chronic situations where people are deprived of basic daily needs as *Roti, Kapda aur Makan* (Food, Clothing and Shelter). If these needs are not fulfilled, then it is understood as violation of Human Rights. Besides these three basic conditions, there are other conditions which corresponds to the violation of internationally recognised human rights standards namely, the right to educational opportunities, the right to health facilities, the right to work, the right to livelihood, the right of equal access to public services and the right to seek justice.

Many countries have got freedom from the yoke of foreign rulers and established *swaraj* in their countries. But today they are suffering from acute poverty, poor health and livelihood *(Roti, Kapda aur Makan)*. In spite of becoming politically independent nation, they have not gained economic independence. This economic independence is a big challenge for the survival of democracy in universal way through Human Rights. With the exit of foreign rule, the nation became helpless in all fronts of lives. The aid/grants they receive from the developed countries for the common masses were attached with strings. This hampered the process of acceptance of Human Rights in newly formed democratic nations. I consider the economic democracy is more important than the political democracy. The situation in third world countries is very pathetic. Especially in African countries. The poverty is on its peak. Besides in third world countries, poverty lies in significant pockets even in the richer nations like the UK, Canada, Australia and New Zealand.

"Poverty is a condition brought about by people and policies and is not a natural and normal condition. It can and must be changed as a matter of priority. The state of poverty itself, and not the act to eliminate it, is a violation of human rights. Development sees human beings as having needs that should be fulfilled as far as possible."[5]

Many African countries, for example, South Africa and Uganda have recognised the human rights to food, housing, healthcare, education and a clean and safe environment by writing them into their constitutions as fundamental rights that the State is legally obligated to provide for all citizens. In other countries like India and Bangladesh where non-binding constitutional directives to achieve similar goals exist, the judiciary has expanded the scope of the fundamental right to life to include some of these basic entitlements indispensable for the enjoyment of a life of dignity.

Nexus between Democracy and Human Rights

Human rights and democracy are interconnected. A truly democratic society is one in which all human rights, as adopted in the UDHR, are respected and protected. It is through democratic institutions such as an independent judiciary, a military that is accountable to the (democratically elected) civilian government, and a free and responsible press that these fundamental principles are realised. A mere holding periodic election is insufficient. It requires more than that. Human rights operate to limit the laws, policies and practices that can be pursued by governments, irrespective of the way in which those governments achieved and continue to maintain power. True democracy goes much deeper than the electoral process and requires much more work. It would be a serious mistake to imagine that freely elected governments are a guarantee of individual rights or that majority rule can be equated with democratic rule.

Recent history has also confirmed that democracy – as a concept and as a pattern of government – cannot be successfully imposed from outside. For democracy to take root and be flourished there must be common understanding, common agreement and an internal will to change and succeed without any violence. Nepal had a long process of undertaking democratic process. International community has a vital role in building the foundations for a democratic society. States can and should be supported in moving towards laws and systems that support democratic ideals. The UN has been supporting in that direction. They can and should be held responsible for protecting and respecting human rights including those associated with the right of democratic governance. The international community also has an important role to play in reducing the violence, poverty and insecurity that threaten the free and complete exercise of democracy and human rights.

The first decade of twenty-first century has forced us to think carefully about what democracy actually means; how and why we should be promoting democracy outside our own countries; and how we can best respond to situations that threaten the democratic foundations of states or the international community. International human rights law provides important guidance on each of these points. It has been especially useful as a framework and reference point against which state responses to threats against democracy can be measured and, if necessary, challenged.

Linkage between Democracy and Human Rights

There is no doubt that there is a link between Democracy and Human Rights. One can find the link between the democracy and Human Rights in Article 21 (3) of the **Universal Declaration of Human Rights**. This article states that;[6]

> *"The will of the people shall be the basis of the authority of government; this shall be expressed in periodic and genuine elections which shall be by universal and equal suffrage and shall be held by secret vote or by equivalent free voting procedures."*

In 1993, at the World Conference on Human Rights, the member states of the UN affirmed that:[7]

> *"Democracy, development and respect for human rights and fundamental freedoms are interdependent and mutually reinforcing. Democracy is based on the freely expressed will of the people to determine their own political, economic, social and cultural systems and their full participation in all aspects of their lives. In the context of the above, the promotion and protection of human rights and fundamental freedoms at the national and international levels should be universal and conducted without conditions attached. The international community should support*

the strengthening and promoting of democracy, development and respect for human rights and fundamental freedoms in the entire world".

The relationship between democracy and human rights is very obvious. However, this was not always the case. As noted above, the Charter of the UN, despite its clear commitment to ideals that we would readily associate with democracy, contains no direct reference to this concept. None of the major human rights instruments, the United Nations, Democracy and Human Rights including the **Universal Declaration** and the two international covenants, make an explicit link between democracy and human rights.

At the same time, there have been many international organisations which show that there has been a link between these two concepts. Organisations like, African Union, the Organisation of American States, the European Union, the Council of Europe, the Organisation of Security and Co-operation in Europe, the Organisation *Internationale de la Francophonie*, the Commonwealth, the United Nations, the Inter-Parliamentary Union, the Community of democracies, etc have seen link between these two concepts. But the most important link can be found in Article 21 (3) of the Universal Declaration of Human Rights.

Since the very inception, the UN General Assembly and the former Commission on Human Rights endeavoured to draw on international human rights instruments to promote a common understanding of the principles, norms, standards and values that should be the basis of democracy.

In 2000, the Commission recommended a series of important practical measures to consolidate democracy (resolution 2000/47); and in 2002, the Commission declared the following as essential elements of democracy:[8]

- *Respect for human rights and fundamental freedoms*
- *Freedom of association*
- *Freedom of expression and opinion*
- *Access to power and its exercise in accordance with the rule of law*

- *The holding of periodic free and fair elections by universal suffrage and by*
- *Secret ballot as the expression of the will of the people*
- *A pluralistic system of political parties and organisations*
- *The separation of powers*
- *The independence of the judiciary*
- *Transparency and accountability in public administration*
- *Free, independent and pluralistic media*

One can find a very significant link between democracy and human rights. One can see this link as, "primarily, the existence of the link is recognised mainly in policy documents generally conceived not to be legally binding upon the participating states. However, it has convincingly been argued that the qualification of a policy document does not necessarily mean that it does not contain any legally binding norms as such documents may contain clauses stemming from international law, referring to international law or can be traced to international agreements by which the participating states are legally bound.

Secondly, a universal consensus exists on the existence of a "link" between these concepts. The nature of that link is not specified and thus, skeptics could rightfully argue that as the wording used is general in nature one could question whether a true consensus does exist on the nature of that link."[9]

The references to the existence of a link between democracy and human rights can be divided into two groups. Some approaches consider respect for human rights to be a prerequisite for democracy, or the other way around. Other approach list that democracy and human rights are interdependent and mutually reinforcing.

Difference between these two approaches

Respect for human rights is often perceived to be a prerequisite for democracy or vice versa. "Respecting human rights is perceived to be one set of various elements, including amongst others -apart from respect for human rights- respect for the principles of the rule of law and separation of powers."[10] Other texts seem to consider respect for human rights as the only requirement that needs to be fulfilled in order to be considered to be a democracy.

Other texts consider democracy to be a prerequisite for respecting human rights insinuating that in a democracy respect for human rights is best assured. If a nation respects human rights it automatically may be considered to be a democracy and a democracy automatically respects Human Rights. In short both go side by side and at the same time both are complimentary to each other.

Another view with respect to these two concepts is, respecting human rights does not automatically turn a nation into a democracy. Certain human rights can adequately be protected in non-democracies. At the same time, one cannot accept that in a democracy respect for human rights is best assured is false. Some time one feels that democracy does not necessarily entail better protection of human rights. Democracy may even exacerbate ethnic conflict and lead to greater violations of human rights especially in the period immediately following transition to a democratic system. One can see in Nepal when people decided to remove monarchical government and adopt constitution for Nepal. There had been wide range of violence in all parts of Nepal. *Madhheshi* (a migrant Nepalese group residing in Nepal for many years) have been demanding a share in a democratic and constitutional government in Nepal. Respect for human rights is only said to increase at the end of the democratisation process i.e., when a democracy is well installed. After many years, democratic pattern has been installed in Nepal.

Role of UN in promotion of democratic governance

We always think that the role of the UN is to protect Human Rights and it is true. But it also helps in the promotion of democracy throughout the world. It is true; the concept 'democracy' has not appeared in the United Nations Charter, still it supports Human Rights. "The very opening word of United Nations Charter document states: *We the Peoples of the United Nations*, clearly linked the legitimacy of this new organisation and its member states to the will of the people. This commitment finds further expression in the purposes of the United Nations that include promotion of universal respect for human rights and fundamental freedoms for all, without distinction."[11]

The UN supports democratic governance and it also emphasizes the role of individuals and people in general in shaping their human growth and human development of societies. In 2011, the United Nations Development Programme (UNDP) helped more than 130 countries and also devoted US $ 1.5 billion in resources to democratic governance. "In 2014, the UNDP strengthened electoral processes around the world and helped register 18 million new voters. The UNDP also works to foster partnerships and share ways to promote participation, accountability and effectiveness at all levels, aiming to build effective and capable states that are accountable and transparent, inclusive and responsive — from elections to participation of women and the poor".[12]

India is among the top contributors to the UN Democracy Fund (UNDEF) whose mission is to promote democracy across the world through local and international NGOs and civil society organisations (CSOs). Since UNDEFs inception in 2005, India has contributed over $32 million to it and remains its fourth largest contributors after US, Sweden, and Germany. India's Permanent Mission to the UN gave a statement: "India acknowledges that sustained support for UNDEF is particularly important in this crucial time for democracy efforts worldwide. India expresses steadfast support for UNDEF as it plays a distinct role in complementing other UN efforts to strengthen democratic governance around the world."[13]

Besides United Nations Development Programme (UNDP), the High Commissioner for Human Rights (OHCHR) also support the democratic governance by providing sustainable support to democratic institutions, such as supporting civil society, facilitating drafting constitution and conducting human rights in the context of electoral processes. Sometime, the UN observer is sent to different countries during the conduct of election. In March 2012, the Human Rights Council adopted a resolution titled "Human rights, democracy and the rule of law," which reaffirmed that democracy, development and respect for all human rights and fundamental freedoms were interdependent and mutually reinforcing. The Council called upon

States to make continuous efforts to strengthen the rule of law and promote democracy through a wide range of measures.

In March 2015, "the Human Rights Council adopted resolution 28/14, which established a forum on human rights, democracy and the rule of law, to provide a platform for promoting dialogue and cooperation on issues pertaining to these areas".[14]

Human Rights in the UN's development work

A great part of the UN's work is concerned with promoting and supporting economic and social development. A significant portion of its budget is spent on the promotion of Human Rights. There has been growing acceptance of the need for a rights-based approach to development assistance by the UN and its subsidiary. A rights-based approach calls for situations to be analysed and responded to not just in terms of political imperatives, needs or development objectives, but in terms of a state's legal obligations to protect and realise the human rights of individuals. "A rights-based approach to development will, it is argued, empower individuals to demand justice as an entitlement, rather than beg for charity. A rights-based approach requires the active involvement of people in their own development. It gives a community the legal and moral basis on which to claim international assistance and to demand a world economic and political order that is respectful and supportive of human rights."[15]

The UN's major development body, the UNDP, as well as other agencies and programmes involved in development (including UNICEF, UNIFEM and UNFPA), have, to various degrees, committed themselves to strengthening support for all human rights and to mainstreaming human rights into their work.

"In September 2000, member states of the UN adopted the Millennium Goal through which they pledged to meet specific development goals (the Millennium Development Goals)."[16]

The goals themselves as well as the plan for their implementation both reflect and reinforce the link between development and human rights. Many third world countries have achieved these goals especially alleviating poverty.

Conclusion

I conclude in emphasizing that democracy and human rights go hand in hand and both are important for each and every country. This means that every human being has a human right to democracy. "We generally encounter an expression democracy and human rights so frequently that this pair of concepts seems almost unbreakable, taken-for-granted, and not deserving reflection."[17]

One can also say that democracy and Human Rights are inseparable and inalienable. Again, question arises, can human rights also be realised in a political and legal system which is not democratic? No, human rights cannot be fully implemented if the political and legal system is not democratic as every human being's participation in opinion-building and decision-making processes is protected by human rights. Democracy and Human Rights go side by side and which means that human rights can be legitimated by democratic processes, but in addition a moral justification which goes beyond the boundaries of national democratic systems is necessary to ensure that every human being – even outside of these boundaries – are holders of human rights. The going hand in hand of democracy and human rights embraces the essential role that human rights play for a democracy as its fundament and its frame of reference. Democratic opinion-building and decision-making processes have to respect human rights. This complex relationship between democracy and human rights shows the need for education in democracy which overcomes the reductionist understanding of democracy to recognize only the will of the majority, the need for human rights education. In today's Information Technology society, where the tenets of religion are getting universally accepted, Ethics and Human Rights must be given importance. It is high time that Human Rights and Ethics should be part of core curriculum of all Under Graduate courses. This will in future ensure the past generation that they have created a spark for peaceful co-existence of future generation. Human rights education will help every human being to know about her/his rights in the democratic set-up. Human rights education is a 'must have' and not a 'nice to have' in today's pluralistic society where human rights enable us to live in peaceful coexistence with respect for the human dignity of each other and with tolerance across the boundaries of traditions, cultures, religions, world views and opinions; where human rights empower the individual to participate in a democratic opinion building and decision-making process; where human rights protect minorities from the human rights-violating decisions of a majority. To conclude I must say Democracy and Human Rights are complimentary to each other. There is an intimate relationship between these two concepts. As mankind makes progress in science and technology the domains will get more extended and they give more visibility. Conscientisation of Human Rights Education and promotion of democracy is the need of the hour.

Notes

1. O. P. Gauba, *An Introduction to Political Theory*, (New Delhi: Macmillan India Limited, 2014) p. 565.
2. http://www.socionauki.ru/book/files/globalistics_and_globalization_studies_3/112-125.
3. Joseph Benjamin, *Human Rights in Indian Situation*, (New Delhi: Indian Social Institute, 2008), p. v.
4. Joseph Benjamin, Poverty and Malnutrition, *Indian Journal of Political Science, Vol. LXXIII, No. 3, September 2012, p. 477.*
5. Commonwealth Expert Group in Democracy and development, http://www.the commonwealth.org/shared_asp_files/uploadedfiles Also see, Human Rights and Poverty Eradication: A Talisman for Commonwealth, 2001, CHRI, New Delhi.
6. www.un.org/en/documents/udhr viewed on 17/11/2016.
7. Anne Gallagher, *Manual on Human Rights Monitoring An Introduction for Human Rights Field Officers* (Norwegian centre for Human rights: University of Oslo 2001), p. 1.
8. www.un.org/en/documents/udhr/ visited on 26/10/2016
9. www.lawteacher.net/free-law-essays/international-law/democracyand humanrights
10. www.lawteacher.net/free-law-essays/international-law/democracyand humanrights
11. Anne Gallagher, *Manual on Human rights Monitoring An Introduction for Human Rights Field Officers* (Norwegian centre for Human rights: University of Oslo, 2001) p. 1.
12. www.lawteacher.net/free-law-essays/international-law/democracyand humanrights
13. *Indian Express*, "India fourth highest donor to UN Democracy Fund", April 11, 2023, p. 1.

14. www.un.org/en/documents/udhr
15. hppt://hdr.undp.org/en/reports/global/hdr/2000/
16. General Assembly Resolution 55/2, *United Nations Millennium Declaration.* Among 8 goals, poverty alleviation was the most important goal adopted by the UN.
17. http://cisr.ru/files/publ/Meylakhs/Meylakhs_UnPubl_HR%26Democracy

7

India's Human Rights Diplomacy

Introduction

For any country, foreign policy determines how countries relate to one another in international relations. The foreign policy ensures that every country is generally on good terms with other states. Every country in international relations formulates foreign policy with other states that ensures that its national interests are fulfilled. Foreign policy is the channel through which countries translate their national interests and try to fulfil their goals. There are many factors which determine any country's foreign policy. These factors are called determinants of foreign policy. There are primarily seven determinants of foreign policy.[1] They are: Geographical location, Population, History, Economic resources, Development, Public opinion, Decision-makers, and Domestic Instability.

The first Prime Minister of Independent India, Pandit Jawaharlal Nehru believed *Panchsheel* as a basis for foreign relation. During a treaty between the Tibet Region of China and India signed on April 29, 1954 he emphasised five virtues for foreign policy, namely; (a) Mutual respect for each other's territorial integrity and sovereignty (b) Mutual non-aggression, (c) Mutual non-interference, (d) Equality and Mutual benefit, (e) Peaceful co-existence. This can be considered as moral aspects of India's Foreign Policy. After this agreement Indo-China war broke out in 1962. Today these aspects of India's foreign policy is not considered as important. Today the main focus on foreign relation is based on national interest. Any country's national interest has to be fulfilled.

The present chapter would focus on India's foreign policy and try to study how India is able to protect and promote Human Rights in India and other parts of the world keeping in mind its national interest. An effort is also made to study various factors in formulating foreign policy with other States which ensures its national interests.

Foreign policy can be defined as a set of principles, decisions and means adopted and implemented by a nation for securing the definite goals of national interests with other nations- through the exercise of national power in international relations. Normal Hill considers foreign policy as the substance of nation's efforts to promote its interests vis-à-vis other nations. Foreign policy always tries to secure objectives of national interest. The foreign Policy can be established with the definite goals of national interest. The national interest can be trade, security etc. It can be also due similar ideology. Pt. Jawaharlal Nehru, the architect of foreign policy perceived a symbiotic relationship between the fundamental elements of human rights and peace. Both are indivisible, inalienable and absolute if considered in true sense of term. Without peace, there is no life; without life, there is no right. The correlation between peace and human rights found clear manifestation in the Charter of United Nations and that of the UNESCO.[2]

Meaning and Evolution of Human Rights

Human Rights are generally defined as the rights which every human being is entitled to enjoy and to have protected. In order to recognize and protect all rights, the United Nations was established as an organisation in 1945. It tries to promote and protect all recognised rights of the United Nations. The idea of human rights can also be defined as, *"entitlements due to every man, women and child because they are humans."*[3]

Human Right has its roots in the thought process of all ancient civilisation and in utterances of various thinkers whether they are from western world or Asian continent. Ancient Greek philosophers gave the idea of equality before law, whereas Roman thinkers developed the theory of natural law. Hinduism always praised the divinity of human souls. Lord Krishna proclaimed '*Samoham Sarvabhuteshu*, that means, I am equally present in all beings.....They abide in Me; and I too stand revealed in them.[4]

Islam also preached love, mercy, compassion and justice as revealed in the Holy Quran.[5] Mahatma Gandhi glorified *Dharma* as service to *Daridra Narayan*-service to the poorest of the poor as God. Karl Marx's communist dream was to usher humanity into the kingdom of freedom for free development of all.[6] The Magna Carta (1215) and the British Bill of Rights (1689) along with American Declaration of Independence (1776) and the French Revolution (1789) were human rights landmarks. Besides these landmarks, other organisation, mainly non-State actors or one can call it as Non-Governmental Organisations (NGOs), have also contributed for the establishment of Human Rights Commission. The NGOs such as the Anti-Slavery Society of Britain was established in 1787. Henri Dunant, who conceived the idea of what became the Red Cross, obtained the support of "Geneva Society for the Protection of Public Interests" and used the International Statistical Congress of Berlin 1863 as sounding board which helped to persuade governments to take initiative which led to the first Geneva Convention of 1864.[7] The present form of Human Rights first got some idea from the League of Nations (1919) and subsequently more particularly the United Nations (1945).

India's Diplomacy and Formulation of United Nations

India believes in buzz words, *Vasudhaiv Kutumbakam,* which means the whole world is one family and this buzz word has become the guiding *mantras* for India's foreign policy. Today these words have expanded its belief during G 20 Presidency, in 2023, focusing on *"one earth, one family, one future.*" India's freedom movement was basically a struggle for human rights as part of the world's anti-imperialism movement of the exploited people. Independent India provided it a place of pride and prominence on its foreign policy agenda to build a humane world through vigorous diplomatic endeavour. After adopting the concept of human rights, the world is trying to interpret the concept according to their own interest. It has become handy to erect trade barriers against unfriendly countries. It is a good sign that there is a growing awareness for humanist ideology among newly independent countries but it is unfortunate that today the concept of human rights are being used/abused as a moral mask to cover the ugly designs of those who have mass-destruction weapons to dominate and exploit the economically weaker countries, especially third world countries.

Independent India has made very constructive contributions in the earlier sessions of the Commission on Human Rights by putting forth number of outputs in a form of very useful suggestions during the drafting and formulation of the Universal Declaration of Human Rights on December 10, 1948. During the San Francisco Conference, Vijayalakshmi Pandit[8] pleaded justice for peace by condemning un-representative nature of Indian delegation through memorandum to organisers and press conference. Speaking in the conference on 24 April 1945, A. R. Mudalier, a leader of Indian delegation, at San Francisco conference, emphasised to eradicate the roots of conflict for stable peace and security. He urged: "*When we are all thinking of security, of armed forces which will prevent aggression, we are likely to forget the basic factor, the cause which leads to aggression. This is an aspect to which my country attaches the very greatest importance. There is one great reality which must be remembered by all of us- the dignity of the common man, the fundamental human rights of all beings all over the world*".[9] It is very important to note that the first independent Indian delegation to an international conference was sent to the United Nations General Assembly in October 1946, headed by Vijayalakshmi Pandit. India raised the issues on racial discrimination in South Africa and the ill-treatment to Indians. The contributions of Indian delegation in the conference was very remakable. Indian delegates proposed four amendments. One of the important incorporations in the United Nations was the promotion of human rights.[10] India placed equal respectability to the ideal of human rights as that of peace and security.

Racialism as Violation of Human Rights

India had been raising the issue of racialism in South Africa for many years. India took a very strong step against Africa's racial policy which adversely affected the life of people of Indian origin in particular and other blacks of South Africa in general. Mahatma Gandhi also experienced the racial discrimination in South Africa. He also protested against the racial discrimination during his stay in South Africa. Since South Africa did not take the cognizance to India's appeal, India recalled its High Commissioner in March 1946, and put economic embargo against South Africa. India decided to raise the issue before the United Nations. A memorandum was presented in August 1946, listing the plights of Indian origins in South Africa.

A high-power delegation under the leadership of Vijayalakshmi Pandit[11] was sent to the first session of the General Assembly. She strongly raised the matter of Indians before the General Assembly:

> *So long as the obnoxious principles embodied in the Asiatic Land Tenured and Indian Representation Act are adhered to, it will not be possible for India to have any kind of relations with South Africa. The question of Indians in South Africa is only a symbol. The real issue involved ...affects not only Indians but all the peoples of Asia and Africa. For us, it is not the mere assertion of certain rights and privileges. We look upon it primarily as a challenge to our dignity and self-respect.*[12]

India succeeded in raising the issue on the international forum and ultimately the United Nations passed a resolution asking South Africa to uphold its obligations under the Charter and bilateral agreements. Issues of anti-colonialism and anti-racialism in South Africa got support from various organisations and Meets. Anti-racial movement was supported through Asian Relations Conferences (1947, 49), Bandung Conference (1955), NAM and Commonwealth summits to assert collectively and to take joint actions at the United Nations. India's consistent effort made the issue of apartheid a permanent feature of UN debate in 1950s. The delegate of South Africa quite often decided to walkout from the debate. Apartheid was considered as a crime against humanity and threat to international peace.[13] Finally, racist white regime collapsed in South Africa (1994) Namibia (1990) became independent after about 50 years of struggle of India and others. And now Botha, the apartheid-era president of South Africa was tried for authorising killings of blacks and other political crimes.[14]

Approaches to International Application of Human Rights

Roger Stenson Clark speaks of three main approaches[15] for international application of human rights. First, on the government-to-government level through bilateral diplomacy or resort by a government to multilateral machinery. Second, to give individuals direct access to an international commission or tribunal. The third approach is through an international executive who can influence governments through fact finding, publicity and persuasion. India follows first and third approaches, it is understood that the second approach is not applicable for India. India has not acceded to the first Optical Protocol to the Civil and Political Rights 1966 which permits individuals under certain circumstances to file complaints against ratifying state. The basic problem with first and third approaches is that they are taken as interference in the internal matters and therefore, the bogey of domestic jurisdiction,[16] which is a stumbling block in global compliance, is often raised. However, a country cares for human rights when it identifies with the victim.[17] This identification with the victim brings subjectivity in the matter. If a friendly country commits mistakes, even that is supported; whereas an unfriendly country is unnecessarily criticised and often the issue is blown out of proportion. And the Indian state is not an exception to this pragmatic rule of the international political game.[18]

India gained its world-wide importance on the cause of blacks in South Africa. India did fight for the protection of rights of blacks and as well as the Indian migrants living in South Africa. India stopped Indians to visit South Africa. Indian passport holders were not allowed to go to South Africa. This was as a protest against violation of human right in South Africa. Racial discrimination in South Africa was considered as a sheer violation of human rights. India imposed economic embargo in South Africa. In a similar ground, India did not say anything when Soviet tanks moved in Hungary to muzzle pro-democratic forces in October 1956.

For any domestic disturbance in India is linked to foreign hand. For example, Khalistani movement in India. Mrs Indira Gandhi quite often accused Amnesty International supporting opposition parties.[19] Even Modi government also accused India Amnesty International on the question of trying to dodge Foreign Contribution Regulation

Act (FCRA) rules, after being denied permission/registration under FCRA by the Union Ministry of Home Affairs. Amnesty was accused of creating a commercial arm called Amnesty International India Pvt Ltd to receive foreign funding in violation of FCRA rules. Former Chief India Amnesty International, Akar Patel was denied to visit US at Bangalore Airport.[20] Mrs Indira Gandhi made an open statement in favour of the Movement for Restoration of Democracy (MRD) Nusrat Bhutto and Badshah Khan in 1983. This was not interference in the internal affairs of Pakistan in her opinion while expressing her views.[21] But when Mujibur Rehman of Bangladesh imposed emergency on 28 October 1974, suspending fundamental rights and ordering all privately owned newspapers to close down; Mrs Indira Gandhi did not see any challenge to democracy. Presidential system was introduced in Bangladesh on 25 January 1975 and Mujibur received congratulation from Indira Gandhi.[22] In her opinion, the US and Pakistan were responsible for the Soviet intervention in Afghanistan and she felt the Soviets were sympathised as helpless to take serious steps. Like most of the strong rulers who were bothered for their own position, she generally sided with expediency ignoring principles. Growing domestic challenges could have received legitimate international support through two Covenants of 1966. Therefore, she did not like India to accede to it. They were ratified when Janata Party was in power in 1979; which came to power fighting her Emergency rule with a promise to strengthen democracy in India. India kept silent when Tinanman square massacre took place in summer 1989 as efforts were being made to normalise relations with China.[23]

Western world has supported the worst violators of human rights. The USA and UK have supported the racist government in South Africa in order to protect their vested interests in South Africa. Pakistani military government were supported by US in the name of containing communalism. Many dictators in the world were friends to America. Zionist Israel is supported by US. Most of the wars taken place in the world with weapons supplied by USA and other big powers causing mass destruction.[24] War in Itself is the most violation of human rights-right to life.[25] Hence, Russian attack on Ukraine in certainly a violation of Human Rights. Western world is criticising Russia where as India is taking neutral role. During

Iran-Iraq war US had put so much sanction on Iraq. At the same time, UN (US) sanctions on Iraq have caused so much misery. Cancer was on the rise. Cancer was being caused by depleted Uranium shells used by the US against Iraq during Desert Storm.[26] This human rights violation can be seen outside the USA. But in domestic social sector also there has been violation of human rights. A survey conducted by a Rutgers University labour economist on behalf of the Associated Press found that 290,200 children, two-thirds of them 15 years or younger worked unlawfully in America in the year 1996-97.[27]

Indian Human Rights Diplomacy

A state's human rights diplomacy may be assertive or defensive.[28] Assertive diplomacy will use a variety of means to influence global human rights practices, agreements, and institutions. It will accuse other states of violating human rights and pursue those accusations in international institutions or in its direct relations with the accused and other states. Assertive human rights diplomacy often entails the implication that the assertive state has superior knowledge and practice of human rights compared with accused states.

The United States and other Western states have been conducting assertive human rights diplomacy with such broad claims implicit or explicit. Pakistan, in spite of many domestic and international problems, has conducted assertive human rights diplomacy against India regarding Kashmir. They are not able to resolve their own problem and have been raising Kashmir issue on world forum.

Defensive human rights diplomacy opposes other states' assertive diplomacy. It usually proclaims state sovereignty and the adequacy of the state's human rights performance under existing local conditions and global agreements. It denies the legitimacy of intrusions by international human rights institutions and foreign NGOs, such as Amnesty International, Human Rights Watch, Civil Rights Defenders, Anti-Slavery International, Global Rights, etc.

Defensive diplomacy criticises other states primarily to question their standing to conduct assertive diplomacy. China's human rights diplomacy, especially after the Tiananmen Square incident in 1989, has been defensive. The United States has pursued defensive diplomacy regarding Israel's actions in its occupied territories of Palestine. Defensive human rights diplomacy may be also the defence of democracy and sovereignty against imperialist or aggressive stratagems disguised as human rights concern, or it may be the use of the state's power and international institutions of sovereignty to protect a programme of human rights violations.

Assertive human rights diplomacy, similarly, can range from being what it claims to be to being imperialism or aggression in disguise. In the Indian case, the post-Cold War period has witnessed very little in the way of assertive human rights diplomacy. Indian rhetoric about human rights violations in Pakistan has been more muted than that of Western human rights organisations. During the Cold War, India had criticised actions resulting in civilian deaths in the course of Western interventions in the third world. Indian rhetoric about civilian deaths during the 1991 Gulf War and deaths due to the economic embargo on Iraq was quite muted.

On the other hand, India and China have arrived at an understanding to undertake joint defensive diplomacy on human rights, each remaining silent about the other's human rights violations. Hence, in the aftermath of the Tiananmen Square incident in June 1989, statements from Delhi avoided the suggestion that the Chinese government had violated human rights. This was the time when these two countries were trying to be closer. There had been a series of officials meetings between Indian and Chinese in subsequent months, and Indian official statements avoided any comment on the incident.[29] China in turn came to India's aid at a crucial vote on a Pakistani resolution about Kashmir in 1994 at the UN Human Rights Commission.

Bilateral Policy and Human Rights

There had been three important bilateral relationships in India's human rights diplomacy since 1989 and they were with the United States, Sri Lanka, and Pakistan. India had refrained from human rights criticism of the United States for either international or domestic actions since 1989, in line with its shift to a defensive posture. Instead, India had sought to moderate US human rights criticism of India. The post-Cold War era had been one of unprecedented US criticism of

India on human rights grounds. Although the level and intensity of US criticism against India were a fraction of those against China and some other states, Indian sensitivity to that criticism was high.

The United States began to criticise Indian counter-insurgency methods in Punjab and Kashmir. It also criticised India for child labour, dowry-murders, and other abuses. On Kashmir issue, the Clinton administration revived the formulation that Kashmir was a disputed territory. A series of American statements in late 1993 and early 1994 were perceived by Kashmiri separatists as indications that the United States was growing more sympathetic to their cause. These statements raised fears in India that the resolve of the militants would be strengthened by them. In the case of Punjab, several resolutions in the US Congress, which came close to passing, condemned India for alleged human rights violations there. These were pressed at the behest of persons in the American Sikh community who had made significant campaign contributions to US Congressmen. American newspapers harshly criticised India's human rights record. The US news-media accounts of Indian human rights issues in the 1990s were sharply negative and was close to Western human rights organisations and other international NGOs human Rights bodies, like Amnesty International, Human Rights Watch, Civil Rights Defenders, etc. The US Congress and administration, like some other developed countries, pressed criticism of India for child labour. The United States has concerned about child labour in export industries, such as carpets, even though these account for a small fraction of overall child labour in India. The United States and other wealthy nations have taken steps to reduce imports of carpets produced by child bonded labour. India had opposed the inclusion of clauses in the General Agreement on Tariffs and Trade that bans trade in goods produced by child labour on the grounds that these would do little actually to reduce the problem and would harm the exports of developing countries.

In 1987, the Indian Peace Keeping Force (IPKF) was sent to Sri Lanka as part of the Indo-Sri Lankan accord. The original intention was for the force to disarm the Liberation Tigers of Tamil Eelam (LTTE) in order to enable political reforms on the island to proceed.

India itself had originally aided the LTTE in reaction to anti-Tamil action and sentiments promoted by the Sri Lankan state. The Tigers chose not to disarm and instead to fight, and the IPKF fought an unsuccessful three-year war against them. Several aspects of Indian human rights diplomacy became entangled with this intervention.

Over the years, India shifted its assessment of the main threat to its ideology in Sri Lanka. Prior to 1987, India had accused the Sri Lankan government of human rights violations against its Tamil minority. After the intervention, the focus of Indian accusations shifted to the LTTE itself. The IPKF was also accused of committing some human rights violations, and India prosecuted some soldiers and defended itself internationally against charges it considered exaggerated.

What is distressing about the Indian decision is not just that it does not serve Indian interests, but that the key reason for the decision was not even the pursuit of national interest but rather narrow domestic political interests: prevent additional ally trouble for the Congress-led United Progressive Alliance (UPA) government. Thus, the Indian government has adopted a key foreign policy decision for the crassest of political motives - to hang on in power. In a brave decision marking the reclamation of foreign policy from narrow political interests, India had abstained from voting on a US-sponsored resolution on human rights situation in Sri Lanka. While India had supported the resolution in 2012 and 2013, the latest resolution was much tougher, calling for an independent investigation into Sri Lanka. The resolution passed with 23 votes for, 12 against and 12 abstentions. India's abstention comes after MEA raised red flags about the resolution, saying it would be creating precedents that would be difficult to withstand. Sri Lanka too had mounted a strong diplomatic offensive with the Indian leadership, including long meetings with the national security adviser, Shivshankar Menon. Pakistan did its best to help Sri Lanka by proposing a separate vote on the operative paragraph 10 (deemed most offensive) hoping to remove it totally from the resolution — it failed 16 votes to 25.

BJP leader Subramanian Swamy congratulated Prime Minister Manmohan Singh for India not supporting the resolution. "I congratulate PM Manmohan Singh for ordering the Indian delegation in UNHCR not to support the dangerous US resolution seeking international probe into the so called human rights violations during 2009 anti-LTTE war by Sri Lanka," Swamy said in a statement.[30]

Indian human rights diplomacy toward Pakistan is highly revealing of the new overall posture. Pakistan has maintained an aggressive posture of accusatory diplomacy toward India with regard to Kashmir. India had accused Pakistan of supporting terrorism in Kashmir and other parts of India, and has held it responsible for human rights violations committed in terrorist actions in Kashmir and elsewhere in India. Yet, India has been muted in its criticism of human rights violations committed by Pakistani security forces within Pakistan. The period since 1989 had witnessed a broad transformation of Indian human rights diplomacy. It has moved from an accusatory approach to a defensive one. This transformation has been caused by both global and national trends.

At the global level, the emergence of uni-polarity led to a changed international regime of human rights. There was a much stronger emphasis on the violations committed by governments of developing countries against their citizens. At the national level, India has gone through a profound multifaceted transformation during the 1990s that has affected its human rights diplomacy in a variety of ways. The economic crisis at the start of the decade was accompanied by crises in its political leadership structure, national unity, and Hindu-Muslim relations. As the decade progressed, India resolved most of its immediate crises and emerged with new structures that replaced the older collapsed ones. Peace has been restored in Punjab. Though again in 2023 few leaders have started raising the issue of Khalistan. Then, the government of India has taken stringent actions against those involved in this movement. Some of them have been arrested. India's human rights and overall security performance in Kashmir has been improved. Now Article 370 is removed. Jammu-Kashmir is no more a full State but bifurcated into two union territories. The improved situation led to a more successful defensive diplomacy in multilateral institutions and bilateral relations. Yet the road back to assertive human rights diplomacy will be a long one for India.

Human Rights in Indian Situation

The issues on Kashmir, Punjab, Insurgency in North-eastern States and child labour have tried to taint the image of India on the human Rights related issues. As of today Central Government has decided to reduce the jurisdiction of 'disturbed areas' under the armed forces (Special Powers) Act, 1958 (AFSPA) in Assam, Nagaland and Manipur. It is felt that under the leadership of Prime Minister Narendra Modi, there has been an unprecedented improvement in the security situation in North-East States and in a historic move, after decade, the Centre from April 2022 had reduced disturbed areas under Armed Forces Special Power Act (AFSPA) in Assam, Nagaland and Manipur.[31] If one looks back on December 4, 2021, six minors were killed when the Indian Army's 21 Para Special Force opened fire at a pick-up truck in Nagaland's Oting village, mistaking its occupants for insurgents of banned National Socialist Council of Nagaland (Khaplang-Yung Aung) group. While six died on the spot, two survived. Seven more civilians and a security personnel died in retaliatory violence that followed. The incident, which caused public outrage in Nagaland, led the National Human Rights Commission to take a *sou moto* cognizance of the killings, and state government to set up a Special Investigation Team (SIT) to facilitate free and fair investigation in the case.[32]

No doubt, India has problems of social plurality, religious minorities, poverty, illiteracy etc. In such a social milieu human rights violation take place easily. But never the less reports are sometime politically motivated and based on biased sources. Quite often it is said that foreign mercenaries are involved in terrorist activities and assisting the elements of secessionism. The year 1980s has witnessed one of the most unfortunate phases in the history of India when the Punjab and Kashmir reeled under the terror of Khalistan and Kashmir abetted by Pakistan. Even today the question of Khalistan is being raised today though not aggressive as it was seen in 1980s. Indian government had taken a very bold step to protect the citizens of India and preserved its territory. Democratic elements in the country itself raised voice against the erring forces and they were punished. The army has punished 88 soldiers for committing human rights violations during counter-insurgency operations in Kashmir and

North-East. The punishment included a death sentence and ten years rigorous imprisonment to six soldiers for rape.[33]

Still then India was targeted by different countries, especially by Western world on the issue of human rights violation. Walley Herger, a US Congressman, a member of Republican Party, (1987-2013) introduced a bill in the US Congress to suspend MFN status for India's alleged human Rights violations, in Punjab and not allowing Amnesty International to visit the state. He also raised the voice that Indian voting pattern against USA is worse than Cuba and totally pro-Soviet.[34] Another Republican Party Congressman from Indiana Dan Burton (1983-2013) also put forward similar resolution.[35] Burton was an anti-Soviet and he was always against India's policy. It alleged that Walley Herger was closely associated with Khalistani movement. On the other hand, our neighbour, Pakistan used meetings of the Commission on Human Rights to denigrate India on Kashmir and at the same time it has been providing training to so many terrorists in camps, who attacked various places in India. Indian Parliament attack, Mumbai attack etc, are the glaring examples. Hence, the present Modi government decided not to have any talk with Pakistan unless it stops terrorist activities in Kashmir valley.[36]

Issue of Kashmiri Pandit is not forgotten. It was on January 19, 1990, when the Kashmiri Pandits were attacked and almost 20,000 Kahmiri Pandits families had to leave the valley. Only 800 families stayed back in Kashmir due to some reasons or the other. After the released film 'Kashmir File' by Vivek Agnihotri has brought back in the minds of people about killing of Kashmiri Pandit. The plight of Kashmiri Pandit and crime against them do not attract the Western world. Kashmiri Pandits had to migrate from their native place and were kept for years in different parts of India in various camps. There are very few Kashmiri Pandit families who were living in Kashmir. A 'White Paper' on Pakistani-sponsored terrorism revealed that it claimed lives of 29, 151 civilians and 5,101 security personnel, caused 4,730 explosions and rendered 2,78,601 persons homeless.[37]

It was in this context the government of India decided to establish its own National Human Rights Commission in October 1993. As of year 2022, 26 States in India have constituted the State Human Rights Commission. Besides National Human Rights Commission, other commissions are working in the same direction and trying to protect the rights of marginalised community. These commissions are National Commission for Women, Minorities Commission, Commission for Scheduled Castes and Scheduled Tribes. The National Human Rights Commission has been working as per the norms and receiving complaints and trying to solve it. In 2020-21, the National Human Rights Commission had registered 74,968 cases on Human Rights violations, while in 2021-22 (till February 2022) the commission registered as many as 1,02,539 cases.[38] It has been receiving so many complaints and trying to resolve it. As such the NHRC does not have the power of prosecution. It is a merely an investigating body. But Indian Judiciary has taken the matter of Human Rights seriously through PIL and Judicial Activism. Hence, one can say that India's democratic structure and its international commitment have obliged it to abide by Human Rights.

Foreign policy assertiveness

India's relations with some of its neighbouring countries have always been problematic. India views China and Pakistan as its biggest security challenges in the region. One can see with Indo-Pak wars and Indo-China war of 1962 and frequent hiccups on Indo-China boarder. This aspect of India's foreign policy has remained unchanged for the past few decades. But security analysts say that unlike his predecessors, PM Modi has chosen to be more assertive when it comes to national security. As an example of this assertiveness, they point to India's "surgical strike" against[39] suspected militant hideouts in Pakistan in response to a deadly attack on Indian troops in Kashmir in February.[40] While Modi received domestic praise for his military action on Pakistani soil, the war-like situation between India and Pakistan was not appreciated internationally. Former Indian ambassador to Algeria, Germany, France and Dy High Commissioner to Pakistan for five years, Mr T C A Rangachari believes that Modi wanted to convey a message to Islamabad that India was ready to talk on the militancy issue but only if Pakistan withdrew its alleged support to terrorists.

Modi's China policy, meanwhile, hasn't succeeded in resolving the tensions and mistrust between the two nations. There has been frequent hiccups on the Indo-China boarder on the Arunachal Pradesh and Galwan Ghat and boader issues. In April 2018, the Indian Prime Minister met with Chinese President Xi Jinping at a bilateral summit in Wuhan. The meeting was touted as a milestone in India-China relations; however it failed to deliver concrete results.[41] Another setback to Indian foreign policy was China's initial refusal to support New Delhi's UN bid to designate Masood Azhar, the head of the Pakistan-based Islamist group Jaish-e-Mohammad, as a terrorist. Beijing eventually lifted its objection on the move on 1st May.[42] China has also obstructed India's entry into the Nuclear Suppliers Group (NSG). It also criticised PM Modi's trips to Arunachal Pradesh, India's north-eastern border state. India firmly rejected China's objection to Home Minister Amit Shah's visit to Arunachal Pradesh and asserted that the State "was, is and will" always remain an integral and inalienable part of India.[43] Even Beijing claims the region, which it calls Southern Tibet, as part of its territory. "While India believes that [international] relations should be governed by principles, China has not paid heed to India's concerns," Rahul Mishra, an expert at the Kuala Lumpur-based Asia-Europe Institute, told DW.[44] Although both China and India have increased bilateral trade and enhanced border control, there is a perception in India that Beijing is unwilling to cooperate on key security issues. New Delhi is also skeptical of China's Belt and Road Initiative (BRI), which it considers a regional security threat. Former Ambassador Mr T C A Rangachari says that India is not alone in expressing concerns about the BRI. "Many countries that have received Chinese loan under the BRI have drowned in debt. Take the example of Sri Lanka's Hambantota port, which has been given to China on a 99-year-lease. If this trend continues, China will occupy territories in the same way former colonial powers and imperialist powers did in the previous century," Rangachari underlined.[45] Still there is a ray of hope on the normalisation of India and China relationship. On 28th April 2023, during the meeting of SCO (Shanghai Cooperation Organisation) all member countries (Defence Ministers Meet) agreed for regional cooperation among all members. Subsequent meeting of member countries of SCO is to continue (Foreign Ministers) where members will be discussing the inclusion of Iran in SCO. Another round of meeting will take place in July 2023 in Delhi.

India's Human Rights Diplomacy during Dr Manmohan Singh

The Issue of civil nuclear deal added to Prime Minister Manmohan Singh's image as a firm leader. After signing the deal, nuclear commercial transactions were concluded first with France, Russia and Kazakhstan rather than the United States. The United States intelligence assessments of India's foreign policy asserted that it will follow an independent path, collaborating with the United States only when India's own interests so dictate.

On another foreign policy issue of the ethnic conflict in Sri Lanka, the election outcome endorsed the voters' acceptance of the ruling United Progressive Alliance's (UPA) careful distinction between terrorism of the Liberation Tigers of Tamil Eelam (LTTE) and Sri Lankan Tamil's welfare and rights. The voters defeated all those extremist forces that went for political mobilisation in the name of the LTTE. After the electoral victory, President Rajapaksa, in his victory speech said, without naming India that no 'foreign formula' will be accepted to address the Tamil political issue. There is also no clarity on the nature of the devolution package to be offered to the Tamils to their satisfaction. India wields very little clout in this context to make the Rajapaksa regime evolve a political resolution of the ethnic issue to the satisfaction of the Tamils and Muslims in Sri Lanka. In Nepal, India has come under strong public rebuke and criticism for siding with controversial army chief against the Maoists and for pushing the Maoist government out. This was a sensitive internal political matter where India could have been well advised to keep a distance. Pakistan is caught in a crisis of its own creation. Its fight against the Taliban in the Swat valley deserves support and encouragement. In principle, it reiterates the Indian position and that of the international community that Pakistan has to fight with the home grown terrorists and stop being a sanctuary for Al-Qaeda and its cohorts. India stopped the peace process and the comprehensive dialogue with Pakistan in the wake of terror attacks on Mumbai in November 2008.

India's neighbourhood includes China as well but China is a major Asian and global power in its own right. As was noticed in the cases of Nepal and Sri Lanka, India's neighbourhood policy is, to a considerable extent, haunted by China. Though China is responsive to constructive economic engagement with India, it was becoming more strident, if not aggressive, on strategic matters. Its assertion of claims on Arunachal Pradesh went outside the bilateral context when, in April 2009, it vetoed an Indian request to the Asian Development Bank for infrastructure projects in that province. In the hope of concretising the G2 dominance in Asia, China proposed to the United States to look after the Pacific region, allowing a free hand to itself in the Indian Ocean area.

Prime Minister Manmohan Singh attended the BRIC Summit in Russia in June 2009. Russia continues to be India's major defence partner. India's engagement with Iran had been restrained in deference to the sensitivities of the Bush administration. Since the Obama administration had a radically different approach towards Iran, India shed its restraints and moved to build a dynamic and mutually advantageous partnership with Iran.

Modi Era and India's Human Rights Diplomacy

In contrast to his predecessor, Manmohan Singh, Modi proved a very enthusiastic traveller, embarking on as many foreign visits during his first term in office as Singh did in a decade, attending a series of high-profile summits, and aiming to establish rapport with his counterparts in China, Japan, and the United States, as well as in South Asia.[46] Modi has had a significant impact on US-India ties, first in setting aside any grievance he might have had about an earlier ban on entering the US imposed upon him, and then in investing effort in building personal relationships with US Presidents, namely Barack H. Obama and then Donald J. Trump. Modi government's shift away from non-alignment and the pursuit of strategic autonomy and the Trump administration's disregard for human rights issues smoothed the road to closer ties, despite missteps by both sides and tensions over trade. The main reason for the improvement of ties was to share concern about Beijing's increasingly assertive behaviour across the region. Modi's China policy, meanwhile, hasn't succeeded in resolving the tensions and mistrust between the two nations. In April 2018, the Indian Prime Minister met with Chinese President Xi Jinping at a bilateral summit in Wuhan. The meeting was touted as a milestone in India-China relations; however it failed to deliver concrete results. This time Chinese President Xi Jinping visited India on October 11-12, 2019.

Modi government has employed a combination of both internal and external balancing, accommodation, and competition to manage the rivalry with China. India also wants that Pakistan should stop sponsoring terrorist activities in India. Like its predecessors, Modi wants to convey a message to Islamabad that India was ready to talk on the militancy issue but only if Pakistan withdrew its alleged support to terrorists. During the SCO meeting on April 28, 2023, Pakistan remained absent.

With regard International relation with Far East countries, India signed a treaty with Japan and sought financial support as well as technological help for Bullet Train between Mumbai and Ahmedabad. Modi's idea of India's Look East/Act East policy and Japan's vision of a 'Free and Open Indo-Pacific' and the efforts made to build formalised dialogue mechanisms and encourage defence and security cooperation between the two. They also outline the extent of the Japanese public and private investment in India, including in major infrastructure projects, as Tokyo aims to boost India's medium to long-term economic prospects. They also explore the burgeoning of mini-lateral coordination and cooperation beyond the bilateral partnership, including under the auspices of the Quadrilateral Security Dialogue (or 'Quad'), which draws in Australia and the US.

After the victory in 2019 election, India has sought for a strategic partnership with other countries. The Indian PM Modi visited Australia, may be the first by any Indian Prime Minister since 1986—raised hopes in Canberra that fast progress would be made both in extending defence and security ties and in negotiating a free trade agreement. In response to Modi's visit to Australia, Anthony Albanese Australian, an Australian Prime Minister made his visit to India in the beginning of year 2023.

Still some Western world feel that human rights are being violated in third world countries. In 2020, UN Special Rapporteurs found that the UAPA contravenes several articles of the Universal Declaration of Human Rights and the International Covenant on Civil and

Political Rights.[47] A key criticism of this law is that it is extremely difficult for those charged to be granted bail. Before 2014, the year Modi was elected, the use of the UAPA law was negligible. Between 2014 and 2020 over 10,000 people have been arrested under this law. Thousands have been under pre-trial detention for years. The Public Safety Act is misused in a similar way.[48]

In response to the question with regard to violation of rights of minorities, especially the Indian Muslims, the Indian Finance Minister, Mrs Nirmala Sitaraman said that the Muslims are growing in India. She was replying to the press conference at the Peterson Institute for International Economic during her US visit on 10th April 2023. She said, "To say it's all the blame of the government of India, I would like to say then, between 2014 and today, has the population dwindled, has the debts been disproportionately high in any one particular community." [49]

Conclusion

According to the fast changing world the concept of human rights has to be re-defined and re-understood. Earlier rights of individual put restrain on state but today rights are goals to be fulfilled and achieved by the state. For example, if we talk of right to education, it cannot be achieved without the support of state. Similarly, the right to life cannot be enjoyed without the support of state. Hence, state cannot be condemned as opposed to human rights. The role of State is very important for the enjoyment of rights. All rights can be fulfilled in a state and by the state. A nation requires to balance between the promotion of national interest and faith in human rights. Therefore, there is a need to make experiments domestically which would automatically be amplified externally as foreign policy and diplomatic behaviour.

India's faith on United Nations and its subsidiaries and other international bodies grew more due to its socio-economic and cultural purpose and programmes. They are considered real domains of necessary actions towards a world wherein all human beings could enjoy their rights as being human which are enshrined in the Universal Declaration of Human Rights. After all, human rights are basically a faith, principle, to serve as a common standard of achievement for all human beings and global world. It is mere a condition for the development of personality which can only be fulfilled by State. Hence, India's contribution towards humanist world will increase if all nations collectively work in that direction as it is not only a national universal pursuit. It should be an effort of all nations, especially member countries to work together for the realisation of basic rights. Yet the road back to assertive human rights diplomacy will be a long one for India.

Notes

1. https://thediplomaticinsight.com/diplomacy-and-foreign-policy
2. Indra Mohan Jha, "Human Rights and India's Foreign Policy", in A. P. Vijapur and Kumar Suresh, ed, *Perspectives on Human Rights,* (New Delhi: Manak Publication, 1999) p. 375.
3. *The Encyclopaedia of Human Rights* (Washington: Taylor and Francis, 1996) p. XIX.
4. Bhagwat Geeta, IX (29).
5. A. J. Arberry, *Aspects of Islamic Civilisation* (London: George Allen & Unwin, 1964), pp. 49-52.
6. *Fundamentals of Marxist-Leninist Philosophy* (Moscow: P. P. H., 1985), pp. 49-52.
7. Roger Stenson Clark, A United Nations High Commissioner for Human Rights (The Hague: Martinus Nijhoff, 1972), p. 5.
8. She led an "un-official" delegation to the San Francisco Conference where the Charter of the United Nations was being drafted in 1945.
9. M. S. Rajan, *United Nations and World Politics* (New Delhi: Har-Anand Pubs., 1995), p. 314.
10. *Ibid.,* M. S. Rajan, *United Nations and World Politics*, p. 320.
11. She was elected the first women President of UN General Assembly.
12. S. L. Poplai, ed., *Selected Documents on Asian Affairs: India 1947-50*, Vol. II. (Bombay: O. U. P., 1959) p. 575.
13. Indian Government did not allow passport holder to visit South Africa as a mark of protest against apartheid in South Africa.
14. *Times of India* (New Delhi), 17 April 1998.
15. Roger Stenson Clark, A United Nations High Commissioner for Human Rights (The Hague: Martinus Nijhoff, 1972, p. XI).
16. John Corey, *International Protection of Human Rights*, (New York: Oceana Pubs., 1968), p. 47.
17. *Ibid.,* John Corey, *International Protection of Human Rights*, p. 46.

18. *Op. cit.*, Indra Mohan Jha, "Human Rights and India's Foreign Policy", in A. P. Vijapur and Kumar Suresh, ed, *Perspectives on Human Rights,* p. 384.
19. *Statesman* (New Delhi) 1 March 1977.
20. *Indian Express,* April 7, 2022.
21. *Indian Express* (New Delhi) 29 October 1983.
22. *Indian Express* (New Delhi) 29 October 1983.
23. Op. cit., Indra Mohan Jha, "Human Rights and India's Foreign Policy", in A. P. Vijapur and Kumar Suresh, ed, *Perspectives on Human Rights,* p. 385.
24. Op. Cit., Indra Mohan Jha, "Human Rights and India's Foreign Policy", in A. P. Vijapur and Kumar Suresh, ed, *Perspectives on Human Rights,* p. 385.
25. ICJ Review (Geneva), no. 57, December 1996.
26. *Times of India*, 7-8 April 1983.
27. *Times of India*, 15 December 1997.
28. Sanjoy Banerjee, "India's human rights diplomacy: Crisis and transformation", in David P. Forsythe, ed., *Human Rights and Comparative Foreign Policy: Foundations of Peace* (United Nations University, 2000), p. 1.
29. Indian Ministry of External Affairs, *Foreign Affairs Record*, Vol. 35, 1989.
30. *The Economic Times*, March 27, 2014.
31. *Indian Express*, 26 March 2023, p. 1.
32. *Indian Express*, April 16, 2023, p. 1.
33. *Times of India*, (New Delhi), 3 July 1997.
34. *Times of India*, (New Delhi), 11 April 1989.
35. *Hindustan Times*, 16 May 1990.
36. Atal Bihari Vajpai government took initiative to normalize the foreign policy with Pakistan. For example, one can still remember his initiatives, like Lohore Bus Journey, Agra Summit etc. but nothing good happened. Kargil attack started by Pakistan in 1997, also see, Joseph Benjamin, *"Indo-Pak Relations A Case of Kargil Intrusion*", in Joseph Benjamin ed, Indo-Pak Relations Prospect and Retrospect, New Delhi: Reference Press, New 2004), pp. 90-118.
37. *Times of India*, (New Delhi), 30 October 1998.
38. See NHRC report.
39. https://www.dw.com/en/indian-strike-targets-suspected-militant-camps-pakistan/
40. https://www.dw.com/en/t-camps-in -pakistan/
41. https://www.dw,com/en/why-is-china-blocking-theterrorist-designation-of-a-pakistani-militant
42. https://www.dw.com/en/mansood-azhars-blacklisting-likely-to-benefit-modi-bjp-in-india-election

43. *The Hitavada*, (Nagpur), April 12, 2023, p.10.
44. https://www.taiwannews.com.tw/en/news/.
45. https://www.dw.com/en/how-pm-modi-changed-the-face-of-indian-foreign-policy/
46. https://www.ncbi.nlm.nih.gov/pmc/articles/PMC8556799/
47. https://spcommreports.ohchr.org/tmresultsbase/downloadpublic-communication.
48. https://theleaflet.in/un-high-commissioner-for-human-rights-criticises-indian-govts-misuse-of-uapa/also see, the *Leaflet* September 14, 2021.
49. *Indian Express*, Nagpur, April 12, 2023, p. 7.

8

Christian Minority and Human Rights

Introduction

Harold Laski has rightly said, "Rights, in fact are those conditions of social life without which no man can seek, in general to be himself at his best." It means rights are essential conditions of good life without them human personality cannot develop. That's why the struggle for the recognition of human rights and struggle against political, economic, social, cultural oppression, injustice and inequalities, have been an integral part of the history of all human society. By virtue of being member of human species, every human being is entitled to enjoy the basic rights. Neither society nor human species can develop without Human Rights. The development of any society depends on human rights.

As Karl Marx asserted, "The History of all hitherto existing society is the history of class struggle." We may say that Magna Carta (1205), Bills of Rights (1648) marks the beginning of struggle for human rights. After World War I & II, the United Nations General Assembly adopted the Universal Declaration of Human Rights on 10th December 1948. The Universal Declaration of Human Rights was not legally binding on countries because it was a statement of intent or principle.

After the Vienna Declaration (1993) in which, 171 countries and hundreds of NGOs participated, accepted democracy as a sole guarantor of individual rights. After Universal Declaration of Human Rights many countries have inserted various provisions for the protection, promotion of Human Rights in their constitution. The UN Declaration of Human Rights also influenced judicial bodies. Since many countries are the signatories of the UN Charter of Human Rights, they try their best to incorporate the basic principles of Human Rights in their educational curriculum.

Human rights are generally defined as the rights, which every human being is entitled to enjoy and to have protected. The struggle for the recognition of human rights and the struggle against political, economic, social and cultural oppression, against injustice and inequalities, have been an integral part of the history of all human society. The conception of the rights, which every human being is entitled to enjoy by virtue of being a member of the human species, has evolved through history.[1]

Now in India, Human Rights education has become the integral part of education system. After the Universal Declaration of Human Rights, it has become the duty of every individual and every organ of society to strive by teaching and education to promote and respect human rights. Human Rights education has become a part and parcel of the goals and objectives of education. Now its components have to be reflected in our university curriculum framework.

The term minority refers to groups and sections of society which number less than the majority, not in the political concept but in the purely demographic sense. In India the Hindus constitute the majority while other communities like the Muslim, Sikhs, Christians, Buddhists, Parsis, Jains and Zoroastrianism form the minorities. The happiness and welfare of these minority communities should be the responsibility of the majority community who in view of the number constitute the ruling class of the country. As their interest are either ignored or given insufficient attention, seeds of discord and disharmony prevail in times of real or imagined conflict and this leads to man-made catastrophe in India. Jawaharlal Nehru, the first Prime Minister of Independent India made some significant observations on the status of minorities. "Many of us are apt to imagine that India is particularly unfortunate in having to face a complicated problem of minorities and different communities. As a matter of fact many other countries have faced and solved this problem." The present chapter would try to study the problems of *Dalit* Christians in India and study their fight for their equal rights in Indian Social system. *Dalit* Christian is denied social justice since Independence. Many Church leaders feel that *Dalit* Christian must be given constitutional safeguards as given to other religious minorities in India.

Christians in India

Jesus Christ founded Christianity, which spread throughout the Roman Empire where it was made the State religion in the 4th century A.D. during the rule of Emperor Constantine. But in India Christianity is said to have arrived during the 1st century after the birth of Christ. Evidence suggests that one of Christ's Apostles, Thomas, reached India in 52 C.E. and settled in Malabar (Kerala). It is said that Jesus Christ Himself sent Thomas. He founded the Church in Malabar. Thomas founded the Mesopotanian Church. It is widely believed that he was martyred in Tamil Nadu in 72 A.D. and was buried in Mylapore, a suburb of Madras, where the Cathedral of St. Thome (built in 16th century) now stands. A rocky hill near Madras Airport is known as St. Thomas' Mount. Syrian Christian arrived in Kerala in the 6th A.D. in a major missionary movement. The Portuguese brought a fresh development, introducing Roman Catholicism. From 16th century till the expansion of Mughals under Chengiz Khan, Nestorian missionaries enterprise were the dominant feather in Asia and the remnant of which in India can still be found in Kerala. Another interesting community of West Asian Christian, who have settlements and congregation in India and have come down to our own times, is the Armenians.[2] The real expansion of Christianity began with the advent of Portuguese in the 16th century. A Jesuit missionary, Francis Xavier came to Goa in 1542 and in 1557 Goa got its first Archbishop named Archbishop Ric. The work of Francis Xavier and early missionaries was confined mainly to the lower classes inhabiting the coast and thought Christianity was firmly established by these missionaries all along the regions dominated by Portuguese influence extended only to a negligible part of the country and the rest part of the country even in the south, remained aloof from Christian influence. It was noticed that the conversion of the lower classes was leading to a general feeling in India that Christianity was a religion, good enough for Parangis and outcastes but not for high caste respectable Indians. In the early stages, the churches were quite influenced by the castes system and the Kerala Christians adopted social rules very similar to high caste Hindus. It was only in the late 18th century that attempts were made to abolish discriminations on the basis of caste. Christians in every State are in minority, except some of the States of the North – East. Now the total population of the Christians is showing some decline. If we take up the case of North India, the percentage of the Christians are on the downfall.

Akbar Court and Christian Missionary

It was the year 1579, when a messenger came at the Jesuit College of St Paul at Goa with a letter from the Mughal Emperor, Jalaluddin Muhammed Akbar in which he expressed his desire to study the teachings of Christianity. In a letter he said, "I am sending Abdullah, my Ambassador and Dominic Perez (an American Christian, the interpreter) with a request that you will send me two learned Fathers and the books of Law, especially the Gospel, that I may know the Law and its excellence..." It was decided therefore, to accept the invitation and three Jesuits namely, Father Rudolfo Aquaviva (who led the mission) Father Antonio Monserrate and the Persian-born Brother Fransisco Henriques were sent to the Court of Akbar. They reached Fatehpur Sikri via Surat and Gwalior in February 1580 and were received with extraordinary warmth and affection by Emperor Akbar. These Jesuits were allowed to furnish a chapel for Christian prayers and to teach without any restrictions. Father Monserrate was made tutor to Emperor's second son Murad, then a young boy. Akbar himself had frequent conversations with them on religious topics and he welcomed their teachings. It really seemed as if he were convinced of the truth of Christianity and on the point of becoming a Christian; but whenever they urged that he should, he drew back, though he took their admonitions in good part. As they got to know him better, they realized that, although his curiosity and zest for religious discussion were boundless, and he was ready to accept ideas from other faiths, he had no serious intension of becoming a Christian. His actual belief was a mystery; he seemed to be interested in several religions, like Hinduism, Jainism and Zoroastrianism as well as Christianity, but to adhere to none. The only thing definite was his reaction for and dislike of Islam, which he showed more and more openly as he overcame his enemies and got absolute power. Thereafter he promulgated a new religion called the *Din Ilahi* combining the elements of all faiths in his dominions.[3] The Jesuits left for Goa in 1583. The second Jesuits team was sent to Akbar Court in 1590 but then retuned back in disguise. A third mission began in 1595, and from then onwards there were Jesuits in at the Mughal Court for the rest of that dynasty's rule. But the Jesuits mission at the Mughal Court laid the foundation for the widely spread of Jesuits networks in India.

Christianity in India Today

Christianity is India's third largest religion with about 26 million adherents, making up 2.3 percent of the population as of the 2011 census. While the propaganda is made through various channels about conversions by missionaries, the population census tells a different tale. As per census figures, Christian population in India was as follows: in 1971-2.60%, 1981-2.44%, 1991-2.34%, 2001-2.30%, and in 2011-2.30%. In fact, the Christian population is on decline if one sees the Census of India from 1971 to 2011.

Christians are mainly concentrated in different states like Kerala, Goa and many parts of North-East States. Religion-wise, Christians are in Minority in India. If one sees the state-wise data, Christians (includes all denominations) are in Majority in few States. Among all seven sisters State, Christians are in Majority or Significant or one can see the plurality of their population. Kerala is the State where St. Thomas, the disciple of Jesus Christ came to this state and propagated Christianity. Today in this State their population is more or less significant, i.e., 18.38%. Again, in North-East, way back in 1921 Salesians of Don Bosco came as missionaries and landed in Guwahati. From Guwahati they moved on to Shillong. It is believed that an English Missionary, William Carey came to Calcutta in 1779 and established his mission in Serampore, Calcutta, and other places. It is also said that he moved on to North-East State that time. During the 19th century, several American Baptist missionaries arrived in the North-eastern parts of India. In 1876, Dr. E. W. Clark first went to live in a Naga village, and started his missionary work. Rev. and Mrs. A.F. Merrill arrived in India in 1928 and worked in the southeast section of the Garo Hills. Rev. and Mrs. M.J. Chance spent most of the years between 1950 and 1956 at Golaghat working with the Naga and Garo tribes. Even today the heaviest concentrations of Christians in India continue to be in the Northeast among the Nagas, Khasis, Kukis, and Mizos. Goa is a state where Portuguese arrived and started ruling. St. Francis Xavier, a Jesuit missionary came to Goa and started his work.

Table 1: Indian States with Christian majority or plurality (2011 Census)

States	Christian Population	Percentage	Status
Kerala	6141267	18.38	Significant
Meghalaya	2,213,027	74.59	Majority
Nagaland	1,739651	87.93	Majority
Manipur	1,179043	41.29	Plurality
Mizoram	956,331	87.16	Majority
Arunachal Pradesh	418,732	30.26	Plurality
Goa	366,130	25.10	Significant

Source: https://en.wikipedia.org/wiki/Christianity_in_India

Dalit Christian and Fight for equality.

If a *Dalit* Hindu converts to Christianity, he forfeits all reservation benefits; if he converts back to the Scheduled Castes, the reservations benefit also return. But the problem should not have arisen at all if the Christian leaders in the initial formation of Indian State would have asked for this special privilege from the first Prime Minister of India, Jawaharlal Nehru. When Pandit Nehru was compiling the list of Scheduled Castes, he called three prominent Christian leaders, namely, Rajkumari Amrit Kaur, Fr Jerome D'souza and Mr. H.C. Mukherjee to ask if any section of their community should be included in the schedule.

They, however, said, "NO". So Pandit Nehru thought that no such measure was needed. After all, Christianity was an egalitarian and classless and casteless religion. Therefore, *Dalit* Christians were not included in the list of the Scheduled Castes.

Further, the administrative fiat that persons who are deemed to have lost caste on conversion to non-Hindu religions (say, Christianity) regain the same caste on re-conversion to Hinduism; remain a paradox, militating against all reason! It is equally a paradox, that Christians of Scheduled Castes origin should be excluded from eligibility to Scheduled Castes status and privileges, on the ground of religion only, ignoring the undisputed evidences of their social, educational and economic backwardness, which qualify them for State protection and reservation policy benefits. It is unfair to exclude *Dalit* Christians from reservations.

The Christian of Scheduled Castes origin should be given Scheduled Caste status and privileges so that they can enjoy the political rights and socio-economic benefits as these are enjoyed by other Scheduled Castes.

Who is a Scheduled Caste? It has been defined in Article 366, sub-article 24 which says: *'Scheduled Caste' means such castes, races or tribes or parts of or groups within such castes, races or tribes as are deemed under Article 341 to be Scheduled Castes for the purposes of this Constitution of India.*

This means that the caste, race or tribe or a part of a caste, race or tribe, will be "Scheduled Caste" if the President in exercise of his power under Article 341 notifies.

Every Hindu, every Sikh, every Buddhist who comes within that Schedule in which the sub-castes have been described will be a Scheduled Caste. 'Scheduled Castes' are not 'castes' in strict legal and lexical terms. They are a category, a schedule, under which the President of India has been empowered to declare any caste, race or tribe or part of a group within any caste, race or tribe as a scheduled caste according to Article 341 of the Indian Constitution.

This certainly does not prevent the recognition of Scheduled Castes converts to Christianity as Scheduled Castes and their inclusion in the lists of Scheduled Castes. The Christian community in general and newly converted *Dalit* Christians in particular have launched their protest at the highest corridors of powers for equal treatment and justice to be given to them. In context of this, the Catholic Bishops' Conference of India (CBCI) met at Tiruchirapally in January 4-14, 1982 and considered the question of caste and its baneful efforts both on society at large and within the Church. At the same time Church of North India (CNI) has noted the cause of *Dalit* Christians in its conclave of October 6-10, 1992 and observed that the fundamental rights of *Dalit* Christians should be restored as per the Presidential Order of 1950.[4] The Members of Parliament had pointed out in the Rajya Sabha debates of May 7-8, 1990 and emphasized that the Scheduled Castes professing Christianity are of the same stock, have the same problem, the same discrimination and the same exploitation. Mrs. Margaret Alva (Former MP), during the Parliamentary Debates in Rajya Sabha on May7-8, 1990 said:

> ..... *I am just raising a point that the Constitution (Scheduled Castes) Order 1950 Amendment Bill is coming up tomorrow. Today, there are no special Motions. We have been asking for long time that in this Order, the Scheduled Caste Christians should also be included. There have been Memoranda submitted to the President, to the Prime Minister and the Home Minister and many political parties also feel that there should be no discrimination based on religion, on this issue, I am appealing to the government since there is a general agreement among most parties that they should also be included in this Order. They may consider this request before they introduce the Bill finally tomorrow.*

On the similar line Shri Subramaniam Swamy, MP said: *"If Buddhist can be included, Christian should also be included."*

During the debate in the Rajya Sabha on the Bill, which was passed and made into an Act in May, 1990 and Neo-Buddhists were listed in the schedule caste list, and the more recent intervention on the similar question in August 1993, have emphasized the deplorable condition of *Dalit* Christians and many stalwarts among the Members of Parliament had urged the government to concede their demands and grant them Scheduled Caste status and provide other privileges.

In fact, earlier Christian leaders, who did not press for the inclusion of *Dalit* Christians in the list of Scheduled Castes, were basically wrong. *Dalit* Christians in India believe they are still carrying the Cross of humiliation, exploitation, oppression and subjugation. When

60 percent of the Christian population, which forms 2.3 percent of India's total population includes such people in North India is as high as 90 percent and another 20 percent came from tribal backgrounds, make a rather disappointed mock of humanity. In Kerala, for instance, the first century converts to Christian faith, the Syrian Christians, were Brahmins. In the South, the first-generation Christian coverts were from high castes. An Italian Jesuit missionary Fr. Roberto De Nobili started conversion of higher castes to Christianity. Later on, when mass conversions, mostly lower caste and low-class Hindus (*Dalit* Hindus) to Christianity, the Brahmin Christians opposed vehemently against such conversions. In Punjab, many upper castes convert to Christianity returned to their original faith of Brahmanism as a result of inclusion of low caste Hindus into Christianity. Brahmin Christians resented when foreign missionaries brought in "sweepers" in mass into Christian congregation.

Dalit Christians are not only recognized by their castes (or no-caste status) but also by their adopted religion due to conversion to Christianity. Thus, they belong to the oppressed class. They are qualitatively different from their oppressors who are identified as upper caste or elite-class.

It is usually said that economic considerations have been put forward as one of the main motives for *Dalit*s to change their religion but this assumption is not wholly true. The economic condition of *Dalit* converts at present is in no way different from that of their counterparts, the *Dalit* who are not converts. *Dalit* Christians suffer from economic and social disabilities and incidence of atrocities to government discriminatory reservation policy.

Disgruntled *Dalit* Christians across the nation are questioning the Church leaders. Some of these leaders, who have been able to overcome the opposition from their upper-class laity, are organizing rallies and *dharnas* demanding the inclusion of *Dalit* Christians in the list.

The Mandal Commission accepts this and recommends 0.58 percent reservation for lower class convert to Christianity. Though States like Karnataka, Kerala, Goa, Tamil Nadu and Pondicherry offer benefits, the overriding problem is of civil rights protection.

There is discrimination across the country and the solution should also be countrywide recognition for their reservation facilities, since they have been carrying heavy burden of segregation on their backs.

When a *Dalit* embraces Christianity from Scheduled Castes, there are two factors in this involvement: Firstly, it is caste, and secondly, it is the religion. But in the case of Scheduled Tribes, this classification and distinction is not there. A person belonging to the Scheduled Tribes can be a Hindu; he can be a Christian; yet they all get reservation and concessions. Thus, religion is not an obstacle in any manner.[5] In Jharkhand most of the tribes are Christians or Hindu and carry tribal surname. Regarding the Scheduled Tribes there is no difference either in caste or religion. But for the Scheduled Castes converts to Christianity, religion comes as a barrier for getting reservations and concessions. Now the barrier of this unsolicited dimension has to be removed so that *Dalit* Christians must be eligible for similar benefits as those of other Scheduled Castes.

A provision in the British India Acts favoured concession for *Dalit* Christians, but since 1950, this concession was not included in the constitution. Their contention is that since they have been continuing in suffering from stigma of untouchability even as Christians, they should not be deprived of benefits as they are entitled to be a backward classes.

However, long before Independence, reservation was in vogue in the erstwhile Madras Province of which Tamil Nadu formed a part. Rev. Fr Jerome himself was from Madras but did speak in favour of reservation of Christians in the Constituent Assembly debates. Hailed as the Magna Carta of the Backward Classes and the under-privileged the Government of India 1919 Act divided the entire population into five groups: viz, Non-Brahmins, Brahmins, Muslims, Christians, including Anglo-Indians, and Backward Classes. Their quotas in government jobs and seats in educational institutions were fixed at 41, 17, 17, 17, and 8 percent, respectively. As far back in 1929, a delegation of Christian depressed classes had deposed before the Simon Commission:

"We remain today what we were before we became Christians-untouchables-degraded by the laws of the social position obtaining in the field, rejected by caste-Christians despised by Caste Hindus and excluded by our Hindu depressed class brethren."

However, that situation has not changed even today. Though the Government of India Act, 1935 did not include *Dalit* Christians in the list of the Scheduled Castes, they did not suffer as they came under the 17 percent quota set apart for Christians and Anglo-Indians.

Drawing the attention to the plight of these less-fortunate people, Mahatma Gandhi wrote in the Harijan on December 26, 1936:

"Whether the Harijan is nominally a Christian, Muslim or Hindu, he is still a Harijan. He cannot change his spots inherited from Hinduism so-called. He may change his garb and call himself a Catholic Harijan, his untouchability will haunt him during his life time."

So, by accepting Christianity it does not mean that the social position is changed.

The Constitution, adopted in 1950 dropped the 1919 and the 1935 Government of India Act and recognised *Dalit* Hindus only as Scheduled Castes. The Constitution was very clear in this recognition:

"No person who professes a religion different from Hinduism would be deemed to be a member of a Scheduled Caste."

Dalit Christians demand an explanation as to why the reservation denied to them. More specifically, they ask why reservation policy is given on the basis of religion at all, giving this to some and denying it to others is discriminatory. *Dalit* Christians constitute 16 million Christians in India. For the past 77 years, this section of Indian untouchables has been discriminated against. The Presidential Order of 1950 and through subsequent amendments thereof to this Order in 1956 and 1990, the Government of India has been consistently discriminating the *Dalit* Christians merely on the ground that they belong to Christian Faith. *Dalit*s belonging to Hinduism, Sikhism and Buddhism are given special privileges on the ground that *Dalit*s are socially, politically, economically and educationally weak. On the same ground *Dalit* Christians have been demanding justice and equality among others. They are not seeking any favour from the government. It is very difficult to find any justification for the government's delay in extending the reservation facilities to *Dalit* Christians.

Denial of Reservation to *Dalit* Christians in 1956

Following an agitation by Master Tara Singh, the Constitution (Scheduled Castes and the Scheduled Tribes) of the Presidential Order of 1950, the Amendment Act 1956 including *Dalit* Sikhs in the list of the Scheduled Castes, was passed in 1956. It said:

> *"Notwithstanding anything contained in para 2, no person who professes a religion different from the Hindu or the Sikh religion shall be deemed to be a member of a Scheduled Caste."*

The Dalit converts to Sikhism protested against discrimination. One of the main arguments they put forward was that many Dalits converted to Sikhism were leaving their religion and joining the Hindu religion to take advantage of the reservation facilities given only to the Hindu Dalits. So, in 1956, Parliament amended the Presidential Order to extend reservation facilities to Dalit Sikh converts.

In the similar line *Dalit* converts to Buddhism also protested against the religious discrimination against them on the basis of religion. After a long time, in 1990, the scope of the Act was futher amended when Mr. V.P. Singh, the then Prime Minister, bringing *Dalits* converted to Buddhism under Scheduled Castes on the ground that change of religion has not altered their social and economic or educational conditions, and that they objectively deserve to be treated as Scheduled Castes for the purpose of various reservations. Para 3 of the Presidential Order now reads:

> *"Notwithstanding what is contained in para 2, no one who professes a religion different from the Hindu, the Sikh or the Buddhist religion shall be deemed to be a member of a Scheduled Castes."*

Thus, for the first time a religious criterion was introduced into the definition of Scheduled Castes. This clearly violated the principle of equality and religious freedom enshrined in the Constitution, Articles 14, 15 and 25.

Dalit Christians unequivocally protested against their exclusion from the reservations and welfare benefits given to Scheduled Castes professing the Hindu, Sikh and Buddhist religions under the President's Constitution (Scheduled Castes) Order of 1950, amended in 1956 and 1990. *Dalit* Christians decried this stand of the Government of India as an act of discrimination based only on the ground of religion is violation of Article 15(1) and contravening the provisions of the Article 15(4) of the Constitution of India. These constitutional principles prohibit discrimination on the grounds of religion, race, caste, sex or place of birth and any disability arising there from, and empower the State to take special provisions for the advancement of any socially and educationally backward classes of citizens or the Scheduled Castes and Scheduled Tribes.

It may be an unpalatable truth, but nevertheless a fact that the SC status for Sikhs and Buddhists was given more for reasons of political expediency and less for reasons of social justice.

Challenge before Church Leaders

Today *Dalit* Christians are asking only for their fundamental rights. They are not demanding the Scheduled Castes status as religious rights but as a social status that is owed to them. *Dalit* Christians too belong to the same caste as their Scheduled Caste Hindus do and go through the same agony and oppression as the others of the same caste. They all belong to the *Dalit* community who are struggling to stand up and claim their legitimate right as the obedient nationals of this great nation.[6] It is said that reservation has been extended to the Scheduled Castes and Scheduled Tribes with the understanding that injustice has been done on a particular section of the society for centuries and they need special help to come up and claim their rightful place in society. *Dalit* Christians also live in the same system of oppression and have been denied real justice and human dignity.[7]

At stake is the fate of 16 million Christians of Scheduled Castes origin, who form 70-80 percent of the Christians in the country (more than 21 million Indian Christians). They are not asking for any expansion of the Scheduled Castes list or an increase in the reservation quota. They only want the Christians of *Dalit* origin to be included in the present list by means of introduction of the new Bill in Parliament. Some people have misconstrued the simple demand for justice and equality by Christians. This clearly violates the principles of equality and religious freedom enshrined in the Indian Constitution, Article 14, 15 and 25, Paragraph 3 of the Presidential Order was supportive to some religious since it provided reservation facilities to only those who professed a particular set of religion and denied the same right to others only on the basis of religion i.e. Christianity.

Conclusion

The Government since long has been ignoring the human rights of *Dalit* Christians. The Church leaders have been fighting for the inclusion of *Dalit* Christians in the List of Scheduled Castes.[8] An attempt was made to introduce a bill for the inclusion of *Dalit* Christians during 1991-1994 but the bill could not see the light of the day. In 1994 again, Welfare Minister had proposed to introduce for the inclusion of *Dalit* Christians in Scheduled castes list. It was approved in the Cabinet meeting and then the Constitution Amendment Bill (Scheduled Castes) was prepared. Although the bill was listed for the introduction as a supplementary item in the Lok Sabha on March 1996, it could not be introduced. Following the adjournment of Parliament, the Cabinet decided that an Ordinance be issued in this regard. An Ordinance was proposed to the President of India, but was not promulgated.[9]

On August 2022, the Supreme Court asked the Centre to clarify governmental stand in the matter on the petition filed by the National Council of *Dalit* Christians and others on the question of listing *Dalit* Christian in the Scheduled List. The Central Government in a written reply said that, "The Constitution (Scheduled Caste) Order 1950 was based on historical data which clearly established that no such backwardness or oppression was ever faced by members of Christian or Islamic Society."[10] Though Justice Ranganath Misra Commission for Religious and Linguistic Minorities had proposed providing reservation to *Dalits* who converted to Christianity and Islam but the Central Government said that *Dalit* who are converted to Christianity and Islam, should not be allowed, since they do not suffer from untouchability. Again on April 12, 2023, when Justice

S K Kaul, was presiding a three-judge bench, questioned while hearing petition, seeking Scheduled Caste status for those who converted to Christianity and Islam, "Can caste be imputed to other religions when the religion does not provide for any such discrimination in its structure..."[11]

The leaders of the Christian community neither felt the need to have a vocal Christian member in the Parliament nor they have thought of forming a political party to strengthen and safeguard the rights and privileges of Christian community as such. It is the need of the hour that all Christian denominations should come together and fight for the rights of Christian community. *Dalit* Christian movement is a struggle for human rights and social justice and this struggle will continue till justice is given to untouchable Christians.

Notes

1. Human Rights: A Source Book, *NCERT, New Delhi* 1996, p. xi.
2. Moore, F A. (1964) *The Christian Church in India Yesterday and today, St. Paul Publication, Allahabad*: pp. 9-13.
3. C B Firth (2005); Indian Church History, ISPCK, New Delhi, p. 110.
4. Shiri, Godwin, The Plight of Christian Dalits, *North India Church Review*, (a Monthly Magazine of CNI) April 2005, p. 4.
5. Banerjee, Brojendra Nath, (1997): Struggle for Justice to Dalit Christians, New Age International Publication, p. 189.
6. Op. Cit Bonarjee, 1997, p. 41.
7. Op. Cit, Godwin Shiri, 1997, The plight of *dalit* Christians, pp. 15-16.
8. *North India Church Review* (a Monthly Magazine of CNI) April 2005, p. 4.
9. S Lourduswamy, *Towards Empowerment of Dalit Christians: Equal Rights to All Dalits,* Centre for Dalit Studies, New Delhi, 2005, p. 113.
10. *Hitavada*, November 11, 2022, p. 1.
11. *Indian Express*, April 13, 2023, p. 1.

Appendices

Appendix-I

Universal Declaration of Human Rights

Preamble

Whereas recognition of the inherent dignity and of the equal and inalienable rights of all members of the human family is the foundation of freedom, justice and peace in the world.

Whereas disregard and contempt for human rights have resulted in barbarous acts which have outraged the conscience of mankind, and the advent of a world in which human beings shall enjoy freedom of speech and belief and freedom from fear and want has been proclaimed as the highest aspiration of the common people.

Whereas it is essential, if man is not to be compelled to have recourse, as a last resort, to rebellion against tyranny and oppression, that human rights should be protected by the rule of law.

Whereas it is essential to promote the development of friendly relations between nations.

Whereas the peoples of the United Nations have in the Charter reaffirmed their faith in fundamental human rights, in the dignity and worth of the human person and in the equal rights of men and women and have determined to promote social progress and better standards of life in larger freedom.

Whereas Member States have pledged themselves to achieve, in cooperation with the United Nations, the promotion of universal respect for and observance of human rights and fundamental freedoms.

Whereas a common understanding of these rights and freedoms is of the greatest importance for the full realisation of this pledge.

Now, therefore.

The General Assembly

Proclaims this Universal Declaration of Human Rights as a common standard of achievement for all peoples and all nations, to the end that every individual and every organ of society, keeping this Declaration constantly in mind, shall strive by teaching and education to promote respect for these rights and freedoms and by progressive measures, national and international, to secure their universal and effective recognition and observance, both among the peoples of Member States themselves and among the peoples of territories under their jurisdiction.

Article 1

All human beings are born free and equal in dignity and rights. They are endowed with reason and conscience and should act towards one another in a spirit of brotherhood.

Article 2

Everyone is entitled to all the rights and freedoms set forth in this Declaration, without distinction of any kind, such as race, colour, sex, language, religion, political or other opinion, national or social origin, property, birth or other status. Furthermore, no distinction shall be made on the basis of the political, jurisdictional or international status of the country or territory to which a person belongs, whether it be independent, trust, non-self-governing or under any other limitation of sovereignty.

Article 3

Everyone has the right to life, liberty and the security of person.

Article 4

No one shall be held in slavery or servitude; slavery and the slave trade shall be prohibited in all their forms.

Article 5

No one shall be subjected to torture or to cruel, inhuman or degrading treatment or punishment.

Article 6

Everyone has the right to recognition everywhere as a person before the law.

Article 7

All are equal before the law and are entitled without any discrimination to equal protection of the law. All are entitled to equal protection against any discrimination in violation of this Declaration and against any incitement to such discrimination.

Article 8

Everyone has the right to an effective remedy by the competent national tribunals for acts violating the fundamental rights granted him by the constitution or by law.

Article 9

No one shall be subjected to arbitrary arrest, detention or exile.

Article 10

Everyone is entitled in full equality to a fair and public hearing by an independent and impartial tribunal, in the determination of his rights and obligations and of any criminal charge against him.

Article 11

1. Everyone charged with a penal offence has the right to be presumed innocent until proved guilty according to law in a public trial at which he has had all the guarantees necessary for his defence.
2. No one shall be held guilty of any penal offence on account of any act or omission which did not constitute a penal offence, under national or international law, at the time when it was committed. Nor shall a heavier penalty be imposed

than the one that was applicable at the time the penal offence was committed.

Article 12

No one shall be subjected to arbitrary interference with his privacy, family, home or correspondence, nor to attacks upon his honour and reputation. Everyone has the right to the protection of the law against such interference or attacks.

Article 13

1. Everyone has the right to freedom of movement and residence within the borders of each State.
2. Everyone has the right to leave any country, including his own, and to return to his country.

Article 14

1. Everyone has the right to seek and to enjoy in other countries asylum from persecution.
2. This right may not be invoked in the case of prosecutions genuinely arising from non-political crimes or from acts contrary to the purposes and principles of the United Nations.

Article 15

1. Everyone has the right to a nationality.
2. No one shall be arbitrarily deprived of his nationality nor denied the right to change his nationality.

Article 16

1. Men and women of full age, without any limitation due to race, nationality or religion, have the right to marry and to found a family. They are entitled to equal rights as to marriage, during marriage and at its dissolution.
2. Marriage shall be entered into only with the free and full consent of the intending spouses.
3. The family is the natural and fundamental group unit of society and is entitled to protection by society and the State.

Article 17

1. Everyone has the right to own property alone as well as in association with others.
2. No one shall be arbitrarily deprived of his property.

Article 18

Everyone has the right to freedom of thought, conscience and religion; this right includes freedom to change his religion or belief, and freedom, either alone or in community with others and in public or private, to manifest his religion or belief in teaching, practice, worship and observance.

Article 19

Everyone has the right to freedom of opinion and expression; this right includes freedom to hold opinions without interference and to seek, receive and impart information and ideas through any media and regardless of frontiers.

Article 20

1. Everyone has the right to freedom of peaceful assembly and association.
2. No one may be compelled to belong to an association.

Article 21

1. Everyone has the right to take part in the government of his country, directly or through freely chosen representatives.
2. Everyone has the right of equal access to public service in his country.
3. The will of the people shall be the basis of the authority of government; this will shall be expressed in periodic and genuine elections which shall be by universal and equal suffrage and shall be held by secret vote or by equivalent free voting procedures.

Article 22

Everyone, as a member of society, has the right to social security and is entitled to realisation, through national effort and international co-operation and in accordance with the organisation and resources of each State, of the economic, social and cultural rights indispensable for his dignity and the free development of his personality.

Article 23

1. Everyone has the right to work, to free choice of employment, to just and favourable conditions of work and to protection against unemployment.
2. Everyone, without any discrimination, has the right to equal pay for equal work.
3. Everyone who works has the right to just and favourable remuneration ensuring for himself and his family an existence worthy of human dignity, and supplemented, if necessary, by other means of social protection.
4. Everyone has the right to form and to join trade unions for the protection of his interests.

Article 24

Everyone has the right to rest and leisure, including reasonable limitation of working hours and periodic holidays with pay.

Article 25

1. Everyone has the right to a standard of living adequate for the health and well-being of himself and of his family, including food, clothing, housing and medical care and necessary social services, and the right to security in the event of unemployment, sickness, disability, widowhood, old age or other lack of livelihood in circumstances beyond his control.
2. Motherhood and childhood are entitled to special care and assistance. All children, whether born in or out of wedlock, shall enjoy the same social protection.

Article 26

1. Everyone has the right to education. Education shall be free, at least in the elementary and fundamental stages.

Elementary education shall be compulsory. Technical and professional education shall be made generally available and higher education shall be equally accessible to all on the basis of merit.

2. Education shall be directed to the full development of the human personality and to the strengthening of respect for human rights and fundamental freedoms. It shall promote understanding, tolerance and friendship among all nations, racial or religious groups, and shall further the activities of the United Nations for the maintenance of peace.
3. Parents have a prior right to choose the kind of education that shall be given to their children.

Article 27

1. Everyone has the right freely to participate in the cultural life of the community, to enjoy the arts and to share in scientific advancement and its benefits.
2. Everyone has the right to the protection of the moral and material interests resulting from any scientific, literary or artistic production of which he is the author.

Article 28

Everyone is entitled to a social and international order in which the rights and freedoms set forth in this Declaration can be fully realised.

Article 29

1. Everyone has duties to the community in which alone the free and full development of his personality is possible.
2. In the exercise of his rights and freedoms, everyone shall be subject only to such limitations as are determined by law solely for the purpose of securing due recognition and respect for the rights and freedoms of others and of meeting the just requirements of morality, public order and the general welfare in a democratic society.

3. These rights and freedoms may in no case be exercised contrary to the purposes and principles of the United Nations.

Article 30

Nothing in this Declaration may be interpreted as implying for any State, group or person any right to engage in any activity or to perform any act aimed at the destruction of any of the rights and freedoms set forth herein.

Appendix- II

National Human Rights Commission, 1993

PRELIMINARY

1. Short title, extent and commencement
   (1) This Act may be called the Protection of Human Rights Act, 1993.*
   (2) It extends to the whole of India. Provided that it shall apply to the State of Jammu and Kashmir only in so far as it pertains to the matters relatable to any of the entries enumerated in List I or List III in the Seventh Schedule to the Constitution as applicable to that State.
   (3) It shall be deemed to have come into force on the 28th day of September, 1993.
2. **Definitions**
   (1) In this Act, unless the context otherwise requires-
      (a) "armed forces" means the naval, military and air forces and includes any other armed forces of the Union;
      (b) "Chairperson" means the Chairperson of the Commission or of the State Commission, as the case may be;
      (c) "Commission" means the National Human Rights Commission under section 3;
      (d) "human rights" means the rights relating to life, liberty, equality and dignity of the individual guaranteed by the Constitution or embodied in the

International Covenants and enforceable by courts in India.

(e) "Human Rights Court" means the Human Rights Court specified under section 30;

(f) "International Covenants" means the International Covenant on Civil and Political Rights and the International Covenant on Economic, Social and Cultural rights adopted by the General Assembly of the United Nations on the 16th 1 * Amended vide Protection of Human Rights (Amendment) Act, 2006 (No. 43 of 2006). December, 1966 [and such other Covenant or Convention adopted by the General Assembly of the United Nations as the Central Government may, by notification, specify"]1;

(g) "Member" means a Member of the Commission or of the State Commission, as the case may be2;

(h) "National Commission for Minorities" means the National Commission for Minorities constituted under section 3 of the National Commission for Minorities Act, 1992;

(i) "National Commission for the Scheduled Castes" means the National Commission for the Scheduled Castes referred to in Article 338 of the Constitution1;

(ia) "National Commission for the Scheduled Tribes" means the National Commission for the Scheduled Tribes referred to in Article 338A of the Constitution2;

(j) "National Commission for Women" means the National Commission for Women constituted under section 3 of the National Commission for Women Act, 1990;

(k) "Notification" means a notification published in the official Gazette;

(l) "Prescribed" means prescribed by rules made under this Act;

(m) "Public servant" shall have the meaning assigned to it in section 21 of the Indian Penal Code;

(n) "State Commission" means a State Human Rights Commission constituted under section 21.

(2) Any reference in this Act to a law, which is not in force in the State of Jammu and Kashmir, shall, in relation to that State, be construed as a reference to a corresponding law, if any, in force in that State.

CHAPTER - II

THE NATIONAL HUMAN RIGHTS COMMISSION

3. Constitution of a National Human Rights Commission

(1) The Central Government shall constitute a body to be known as the National Human Rights Commission to exercise the powers conferred upon, and to perform the functions assigned to it, under this Act.

(2) The Commission shall consist of:

(a) a Chairperson who has been a Chief Justice of the Supreme Court;

(b) one Member who is or has been, a Judge of the Supreme Court;

(c) one Member who is, or has been, the Chief Justice of a High Court;

(d) two Members to be appointed from amongst persons having knowledge of, or practical experience in, matters relating to human rights.

(3) The Chairperson of the National Commission for Minorities,1 [the National Commission for the Scheduled Castes, the National Commission for the Scheduled Tribes] and the National Commission for Women shall be deemed to be Members of the Commission for the discharge of functions specified in clauses (b) to (j) of section 12.

(4) There shall be a Secretary-General who shall be the Chief Executive Officer of the Commission and shall exercise such powers and discharge such functions of the Commission2 [except judicial functions and the power to make regulations under section 40 B], as

may be delegated to him by the Commission or the Chairperson as the case may be.

(5) The headquarters of the Commission shall be at Delhi and the Commission may, with the previous approval of the Central Government, establish offices at other places in India.

4. Appointment of Chairperson and other Members

(1) The Chairperson and [the Members]1 shall be appointed by the President by warrant under his hand and seal;

Provided that every appointment under this sub-section shall be made after obtaining the recommendations of a Committee consisting of–

(a) The Prime Minister — Chairperson
(b) Speaker of the House of the People — Member
(c) Minister in-charge of the Ministry of Home Affairs in the Government of India —Member
(d) Leader of the Opposition in the House of the People — Member
(e) Leader of the Opposition in the Council of States — Member
(f) Deputy Chairman of the Council of States — Member

Provided further that no sitting Judge of the Supreme Court or sitting Chief Justice of a High Court shall be appointed except after consultation with the Chief Justice of India.

(2) No appointment of a Chairperson or a Member shall be invalid merely by reason of any [vacancy of any member in the Committee referred to in the first proviso to sub-section (1)]2.

5. Resignation and Removal of Chairperson and Members3

(1) The Chairperson or any Member may, by notice in writing under his hand addressed to the President of India, resign his office.

(2) Subject to the provisions of sub-section (3), the Chairperson or any Member shall only be removed from his office by order of the President of India on the ground of proved misbehaviour or incapacity after the Supreme Court, on reference being made to it by

the President, has, on inquiry held in accordance with the procedure prescribed in that behalf by the Supreme Court, reported that the Chairperson or the Member, as the case may be, ought on any such ground to be removed.

(3) Notwithstanding anything in sub-section (2), the President may, by order, remove from office the Chairperson or any Member if the Chairperson or such Member, as the case may be–

(a) is adjudged an insolvent; or

(b) engages during his term of office in any paid employment outside the duties of his office; or

(c) is unfit to continue in office by reason of infirmity of mind or body; or

(d) is of unsound mind and stands so declared by a competent court; or

(e) is convicted and sentenced to imprisonment for an offence which in the opinion of the President involves moral turpitude.

6. Term of office of Chairperson and Members1

(1) A person appointed as Chairperson shall hold office for a term of five years from the date on which he enters upon his office or until he attains the age of seventy years, whichever is earlier.

(2) A person appointed as a Member shall hold office for a term of five years from the date on which he enters upon his office and shall be eligible for re-appointment for another term of five years.

Provided that no Member shall hold office after he has attained the age of seventy years.

(3) On ceasing to hold office, a Chairperson or a Member shall be ineligible for further employment under the Government of India or under the Government of any State.

7. Member to act as Chairperson or to discharge his functions in certain circumstances

(1) In the event of the occurrence of any vacancy in the office of 1 Subs. by Act 43 of 2006 for "other members" the Chairperson

by reason of his death, resignation or otherwise, President may, by notification, authorise one of the Members to act as the Chairperson until the appointment of a new Chairperson to fill such vacancy.

(2) When the Chairperson is unable to discharge his functions owing to absence on leave or otherwise, such one of the Members as the President may, by notification, authorise in this behalf, shall discharge the functions of the Chairperson until the date on which the Chairperson resumes his duties.

8. Terms and conditions of service of Chairperson and Members

The salaries and allowances payable to, and other terms and conditions of service of, the1 [Chairperson and] Members shall be such as may be prescribed.

Provided that neither the salary and allowances nor the other terms and conditions of service of2 [the Chairperson or] a Member shall be varied to his disadvantage after his appointment.]

9. Vacancies, etc., not to invalidate the proceedings of the Commission

No act or proceedings of the Commission shall be questioned or shall be invalidated merely on the ground of existence of any vacancy or defect in the constitution of the Commission.

10. Procedure to be regulated by the Commission

(1) The Commission shall meet at such time and place as the Chairperson may think fit.

(2) Subject to the provisions of this Act and the rules made thereunder, the Commission shall have the power to lay down by regulations its own procedure3.

(3) All orders and decisions of the Commission shall be authenticated by the Secretary-General or any other officer of the Commission duly authorised by the Chairperson in this behalf.

11. Officers and other staff of the Commission

(1) The Central Government shall make available to the Commission:

(a) an officer of the rank of the Secretary to the Government of India who shall be the Secretary-General of the Commission; and

(b) such police and investigative staff under an officer not below the rank of a Director General of Police and such other officers and staff as may be necessary for the efficient performance of the functions of the Commission.

(2) Subject to such rules as may be made by the Central Government in this behalf, the Commission may appoint such other administrative, technical and scientific staff as it may consider necessary.

(3) The salaries, allowances and conditions of service of the officers and other staff appointed under sub-section (2) shall be such as may be prescribed.

CHAPTER - III

FUNCTIONS AND POWERS OF THE COMMISSION

12. Functions of the Commission

The Commission shall perform all or any of the following functions, namely:-

(a) inquire, suo motu or on a petition presented to it by a victim or any person on his behalf [or on a direction or order of any court]1, into complaint of

(i) violation of human rights or abetment thereof; or

(ii) negligence in the prevention of such violation, by a public servant;

(b) intervene in any proceeding involving any allegation of violation of human rights pending before a court with the approval of such court;

(c)2 visit, notwithstanding anything contained in any other law for the time being in force, any jail or other institution under the control of the State Government, where persons are detained or lodged for purposes of treatment, reformation or protection, for the study of the living conditions of the inmates thereof and make recommendations thereon to the Government;

(d) review the safeguards provided by or under the Constitution or any law for the time being in force for the protection of human rights and recommend measures for their effective implementation;

(e) review the factors, including acts of terrorism that inhibit the enjoyment of human rights and recommend appropriate remedial measures;

(f) study treaties and other international instruments on human rights and make recommendations for their effective implementation;

(g) undertake and promote research in the field of human rights;

(h) spread human rights literacy among various sections of society and promote awareness of the safeguards available for the protection of these rights through publications, the media, seminars and other available means;

(i) encourage the efforts of non-governmental organisations and institutions working in the field of human rights;

(j) such other functions as it may consider necessary for the protection of human rights.

13. Powers relating to inquiries

(1) The Commission shall, while inquiring into complaints under this Act, have all the powers of a civil court trying a suit under the Code of Civil Procedure, 1908, and in particular in respect of the following matters, namely:

(a) summoning and enforcing the attendance of witnesses and examining them on oath;

(b) discovery and production of any document;

(c) receiving evidence on affidavits;

(d) requisitioning any public record or copy thereof from any court or office;

(e) issuing commissions for the examination of witnesses or documents;

(f) any other matter which may be prescribed.

The Commission shall have power to require any person, subject to any privilege which may be claimed by that person under any law for the time being in force, to furnish information on such points or matters as, in the opinion of the Commission, may be useful for, or relevant to, the subject matter of the inquiry and any person so required shall be deemed to be legally bound to furnish such information within the meaning of section 176 and section 177 of the Indian Penal Code.

(1) The Commission or any other officer, not below the rank of a Gazetted Officer, specially authorised in this behalf by the Commission may enter any building or place where the Commission has reason to believe that any document relating to the subject matter of the inquiry may be found, and may seize any such document or take extracts or copies therefrom subject to the provisions of section 100 of the Code of Criminal Procedure, 1973, in so far as it may be applicable.

(2) The Commission shall be deemed to be a civil court and when any offence as is described in section 175, section 178, section 179, section 180 or section 228 of the Indian Penal Code is committed in the view or presence of the Commission, the Commission may, after recording the facts constituting the offence and the statement of the accused as provided for in the Code of Criminal Procedure, 1973, forward the case to a Magistrate having jurisdiction to try the same and the Magistrate to whom any such case is forwarded shall proceed to hear the complaint against the accused as if the case has been forwarded to him under section 346 of the Code of Criminal Procedure, 1973.

(3) Every proceeding before the Commission shall be deemed to be a judicial proceeding within the meaning of sections 193 and 228, and for the purposes of section 196, of the Indian Penal Code, and the Commission shall be deemed to be a civil court for

all the purposes of section 195 and Chapter XXVI of the Code of Criminal Procedure, 1973.

(4)[1] Where the Commission considers it necessary or expedient so to do, it may, by order, transfer any complaint filed or pending before it to the State Commission of the State from which the complaint arises, for disposal in accordance with the provisions of this Act;

Provided that no such complaint shall be transferred unless the same is one respecting which the State Commission has jurisdiction to entertain the same.

(5)[1] Every complaint transferred under sub-section (6) shall be dealt with and disposed of by the State Commission as if it were a complaint initially filed before it.

14. Investigation

(1) The Commission may, for the purpose of conducting any investigation pertaining to the inquiry, utilise the services of any officer or investigation agency of the Central Government or any State Governmentwith the concurrence of the Central Government or the State Government, as the case may be.

(2) For the purpose of investigating into any matter pertaining to the inquiry, any officer or agency whose services are utilised under sub-section (1) may, subject to the direction and control of the Commission:-

(a) summon and enforce the attendance of any person and examine him;

(b) require the discovery and production of any document; and

(c) requisition any public record or copy thereof from any office.

(3) The provisions of section 15 shall apply in relation to any statement made by a person before any officer or agency whose services are utilised under sub-section (1) as they apply in relation to any statement made by a person in the course of giving evidence before the Commission.

(4) The officer or agency whose services are utilised under sub-section (1) shall investigate into any matter pertaining to the inquiry and submit a report thereon to the Commission within such period as may be specified by the Commission in this behalf.

(5) The Commission shall satisfy itself about the correctness of the facts stated and the conclusion, if any, arrived at in the report submitted to it under sub-section (4) and for this purpose the Commission may make such inquiry (including the examination of the person or persons who conducted or assisted in the investigation) as it thinks fit.

15. Statement made by persons to the Commission

No statement made by a person in the course of giving evidence before the Commission shall subject him to, or be used against him in, any civil or criminal proceeding except a prosecution for giving false evidence by such statement:

Provided that the statement:-

(a) is made in reply to the question which he is required by thr Commission to answer; or

(b) is relevant to the subject matter of the inquiry.

16. Persons likely to be prejudicially affected to be heard

If, at any stage of the inquiry, the Commission:-

(a) considers it necessary to inquire into the conduct of any person; or

(b) is of the opinion that the reputation of any person is likely tobe prejudicially affected by the inquiry;

it shall give to that person a reasonable opportunity of being heard in the inquiry and to produce evidence in his defence:

Provided that nothing in this section shall apply where the credit of a witness is being impeached.

CHAPTER IV

PROCEDURE

17. Inquiry into complaints

The Commission while inquiring into the complaints of violations of human rights may–

(i) call for information or report from the Central Government or any State Government or any other authority or organisation subordinate thereto within such time as may be specified by it:-

Provided that–

(a) if the information or report is not received within the time stipulated by the Commission, it may proceed to inquire into the complaint on its own;

(b) if, on receipt of information or report, the Commission is satisfied either that no further inquiry is required or that the required action has been initiated or taken by the concerned Government or authority, it may not proceed with the complaint and inform the complainant accordingly;

(ii) without prejudice to anything contained in clause (i), if it considers necessary, having regard to the nature of the complaint, initiate an inquiry.

18. Steps during and after inquiry[1]

[The Commission may take any of the following steps during or upon the completion of an inquiry held under this Act, namely:-

(a) where the inquiry discloses the commission of violation of human rights or negligence in the prevention of violation of human rights or abetment thereof by a public servant, it may recommend to the concerned Government or authority –

(i) to make payment of compensation or damages to the complainant or to the victim or the members of his family as the Commission may consider necessary;

(ii) to initiate proceedings for prosecution or such other suitable action as the Commission may deem fit against the concerned person or persons;

(iii) to take such further action as it may think fit;

(b) approach the Supreme Court or the High Court concerned for such directions, orders or writs as that Court may deem necessary;

(c) recommend to the concerned Government or authority at any stage of the inquiry for the grant of such immediate interim relief to the victim or the members of his family as the Commission may consider necessary;

(d) subject to the provisions of clause (e), provide a copy of the inquiry report to the petitioner or his representative;

(e) the Commission shall send a copy of its inquiry report together with its recommendations to the concerned Government or authority and the concerned Government or authority shall, within a period of one month, or such further time as the Commission may allow, forward its comments on the report, including the action taken or proposed to be taken thereon, to the Commission;

(f) the Commission shall publish its inquiry report together with the comments of the concerned Government or authority, if any, and the action taken or proposed to be taken by the concerned Government or authority on the recommendations of the Commission.][1]

19. Procedure with respect to armed forces

(1) Notwithstanding anything contained in this Act, while dealing with complaints of violation of human rights by members of the armed forces, the Commission shall adopt the following procedure, namely:-

(a) it may, either on its own motion or on receipt of a petition, seek a report from the Central Government;

(b) after the receipt of the report, it may, either not proceed with the complaint or, as the case may be, make its recommendations to that Government.

(2) The Central Government shall inform the Commission of the action taken on the recommendations within three months or such further time as the Commission may allow.

(3) The Commission shall publish its report together with its recommendations made to the Central Government and the action taken by that Government on such recommendations.

(4) The Commission shall provide a copy of the report published under sub-section (3) to the petitioner or his representative.

20. Annual and special reports of the Commission

(1) The Commission shall submit an annual report to the Central Government and to the State Government concerned and may at any time submit special reports on any matter which, in its opinion, is of such urgency or importance that it should not be deferred till submission of the annual report.

(2) The Central Government and the State Government, as the case may be, shall cause the annual and special reports of the Commission to be laid before each House of Parliament or the State Legislature respectively, as the case may be, along with a memorandum of action taken or proposed to be taken on the recommendations of the Commission and the reasons for non-acceptance of the recommendations, if any.

CHAPTER V

STATE HUMAN RIGHTS COMMISSIONS

21. Constitution of State Human Rights Commission

(1) A State Government may constitute a body to be known as the .... (name of the State) Human Rights Commission to exercise the powers conferred upon, and to perform the functions assigned to, a State Commission under this chapter.

(2)[1] [The State Commission shall, with effect from such date as the State Government may by notification specify, consist of—

(a) a Chairperson who has been a Chief Justice of a High Court;

(b) one Member who is, or has been, a Judge of a High Court or District Judge in the State with a minimum of seven years experience as District Judge;

(c) one Member to be appointed from amongst persons having knowledge of, or practical experience in, matters relating to human rights.][1]

(3) There shall be a Secretary who shall be the Chief Executive Officer of the State Commission and shall exercise such powers and discharge such functions of the State Commission as it may delegate to him.

(4) The headquarters of the State Commission shall be at such place as the State Government may, by notification, specify.

(5) A State Commission may inquire into violation of human rights only in respect of matters relatable to any of the entries enumerated in List II and List III in the Seventh Schedule to the Constitution:

Provided that if any such matter is already being inquired into by the Commission or any other Commission duly constituted under any law for the time being in force, the State Commission shall not inquire into the said matter:

Provided further that in relation to the Jammu and Kashmir Human Rights Commission, this sub-section shall have effect as if for the words and figures "List II and List III in the Seventh Schedule to the Constitution", the words and figures "List III in the Seventh Schedule to the Constitution as applicable to the State of Jammu and Kashmir and in respect of matters in relation to which the Legislature of that State has power to make laws" had been substituted.

(6) [Two or more State Governments may, with the consent of a Chairperson or Member of a State Commission, appoint such Chairperson or, as the case may be, such Member of another State Commission simultaneously if such Chairperson or Member consents to such appointment:

Provided that every appointment made under this sub-section shall be made after obtaining the recommendations of the Committee referred to in sub-section (1) of section 22 in respect of the State for which a common Chairperson or Member, or both, as the case may be, is to be appointed.][1]

22. Appointment of Chairperson and [Members][2] of State Commission

(1) The Chairperson and [Members][2] shall be appointed by the Governor by warrant under his hand and seal:

Provided that every appointment under this sub-section shall be made after obtaining the recommendation of a Committee consisting of

(a) the Chief Minister — Chairperson

(b) Speaker of the Legislative Assembly — Member

(c) Minister in-charge of the Department of Home, in that State —Member

(d) Leader of the Opposition in the Legislative Assembly — Member

Provided further that where there is a Legislative Council in a State, the Chairman of that Council and the Leader of the Opposition in that Council shall also be members of the Committee.

Provided also that no sitting Judge of a High Court or a sitting District Judge shall be appointed except after consultation with the Chief Justice of the High Court of the concerned State.

(2) No appointment of a Chairperson or a Member of the State Commission shall be invalid merely by reason of [any vacancy of any Member in the Committee referred to in sub-section(1)].[1]

23. [Resignation and Removal of Chairperson or a Member of the State Commission][2]

[3][(1) The Chairperson or a Member of a State Commission may, by notice in writing under his hand addressed to the Governor, resign his office

(1A) Subject to the provisions of sub-section (2), the Chairperson or any Member of the State Commission shall only be removed from his office by order of the President on the ground of proved misbehaviour or incapacity after the Supreme Court, on a reference being made to it by the President, has, on inquiry held in accordance with the procedure prescribed in that behalf by the Supreme Court, reported that the Chairperson or such Member, as the case may be, ought on any such ground to be removed.]

(2) Notwithstanding anything in sub-section (1A), the President may by order remove from office the Chairperson or any [Member][4] if the Chairperson or such [Member][5], as the case may be – is adjudged an insolvent; or

(a) is adjudged an insolvent; or

(b) engages during his term of office in any paid employment outside the duties of his office; or

(c) is unfit to continue in office by reason of infirmity of mind or body; or

(d) is of unsound mind and stands so declared by a competent court; or

(e) is convicted and sentenced to imprisonment for an offence which in the opinion of the President involves moral turpitude.

24. Term of office of [Chairperson and][1] Members of the State Commission

(1) A person appointed as Chairperson shall hold office for a term of five years from the date on which he enters upon his office or until he attains the age of seventy years, whichever is earlier;

(2) A person appointed as a Member shall hold office for a term of five years from the date on which he enters upon his office and shall be eligible for re-appointment for another term of five years;

Provided that no Member shall hold office after he has attained the age of seventy years.

(3) On ceasing to hold office, a Chairperson or a Member shall be ineligible for further employment under the Government of a State or under the Government of India.

25. Member to act as Chairperson or to discharge his functions in certain circumstances

(1) In the event of the occurrence of any vacancy in the office of the Chairperson by reason of his death, resignation or otherwise, the Governor may, by notification, authorise one of the Members to act as the Chairperson until the appointment of a new Chairperson to fill such vacancy.

(2) When the Chairperson is unable to discharge his functions owing to absence on leave or otherwise, such one of the Members as the Governor may, by notification, authorise in this behalf, shall discharge the functions of the Chairperson until the date on which the Chairperson resumes his duties.

26. [Terms and conditions of service of Chairperson and Members of the State Commissions

The salaries and allowances payable to, and other terms and conditions of service of, the Chairperson and Members shall be such as may be prescribed by the State Government;

Provided that neither the salary and allowances nor the other terms and conditions of service of the Chairperson or a Member shall be varied to his disadvantage after his appointment.][1]

27. Officers and other staff of the State Commission

(1) The State Government shall make available to the Commission

(a) an officer not below the rank of a Secretary to the State Government who shall be the Secretary of the State Commission; and

(b) such police and investigative staff under an officer not below the rank of an Inspector General of Police and such other officers and staff as may be necessary for the efficient performance of the functions of the State Commission.

(2) subject to such rules as may be made by the State Government in this behalf, the State Commission may appoint such

other administrative, technical and scientific staff as it may consider necessary.

(3) The salaries, allowances and conditions of service of the officers and other staff appointed under sub-section (2) shall be such as may be prescribed by the State Government.

28. Annual and special reports of State Commission

(1) The State Commission shall submit an annual report to the State Government and may at any time submit special reports on any matter which, in its opinion, is of such urgency or importance that it should not be deferred till submission of the annual report.

(2) The State Government shall cause the annual and special reports of the State Commission to be laid before each House of State Legislature where it consists of two Houses, or where such Legislature consists of one House, before that House along with a memorandum of action taken or proposed to be taken on the recommendations of the State Commission and the reasons for non-acceptance of the recommendations, if any.

29. Application of certain provisions relating to National Human Rights Commission to State Commissions

The provisions of sections 9, 10, 12, 13, 14, 15, 16, 17 and 18 shall apply to a State Commission and shall have effect, subject to the following modifications, namely:-

(a) references to "Commission" shall be construed as references to "State Commission";

(b) in section 10, in sub-section (3), for the word "Secretary General", the word "Secretary" shall be substituted;

(c) in section 12, clause (f) shall be omitted;

(d) in section 17, in clause (i), the words "Central Government or any" shall be omitted;

CHAPTER VI

HUMAN RIGHTS COURTS

30. For the purpose of providing speedy trial of offences arising out of violation of human rights, the State Government may, with the concurrence of the Chief Justice of the High Court, by notification, specify for each district a Court of Session to be a Human Rights Court to try the said offences.

Provided that nothing in this section shall apply, if

(a) a Court of Session is already specified as a special court; or

(b) a special court is already constituted, for such offences under any other law for the time being in force.

31. Special Public Prosecutor

For every Human Rights Court, the State Government shall, by notification, specify a Public Prosecutor or appoint an advocate who has been in practice as an advocate for not less than seven years, as a Special Public Prosecutor for the purpose of conducting cases in that Court.

CHAPTER VII

FINANCE, ACCOUNTS AND AUDIT

32. Grants by the Central Government

(1) The Central Government shall after due appropriation made by Parliament by law in this behalf, pay to the Commission by way of grants such sums of money as the Central Government may think fit for being utilised for the purposes of this Act.

(2) The Commission may spend such sums as it thinks fit for performing the functions under this Act, and such sums shall be treated as expenditure payable out of the grants referred to in sub-section (1).

33. Grants by the State Government

(1) The State Government shall, after due appropriation made

by Legislature by law in this behalf, pay to the State Commission by way of grants such sums of money as the State Government may think fit for being utilised for the purposes of this Act.

(2) The State Commission may spend such sums as it thinks fit for performing the functions under Chapter V, and such sums shall be treated as expenditure payable out of the grants referred to in sub-section (1).

34. Accounts and Audit

(1) The Commission shall maintain proper accounts and other relevant records and prepare an annual statement of accounts in such form as may be prescribed by the Central Government in consultation with the Comptroller and Auditor-General of India.

(2) The Accounts of the Commission shall be audited by the Comptroller and Auditor-General at such intervals as may be specified by him and any expenditure incurred in connection with such audit shall be payable by the Commission to the Comptroller and Auditor-General.

(3) The Comptroller and Auditor-General or any person appointed by him in connection with the audit of the accounts of the Commision under this Act shall have the same rights and privileges and the authority in connection with such audit as the Comptroller and Auditor-General generally has in connection with the audit of Government accounts and, in particular, shall have the right to demand the production of books, accounts, connected vouchers and other documents and papers and to inspect any of the offices of the Commission.

The accounts of the Commission as certified by the Comptroller and Auditor-General or any other person appointed by him in this behalf, together with the audit report thereon shall be forwarded annually to the Central Government by the Commission and the Central Government shall cause the audit report to be laid as soon as may be after it is received before each House of Parliament.

35. Accounts and Audit of State Commission

(1) The State Commission shall maintain proper accounts and

other relevant records and prepare an annual statement of accounts in such form as may be prescribed by the State Government in consultation with the Comptroller and Auditor-General of India.

(2) The accounts of the State Commission shall be audited by the Comptroller and Auditor-General at such intervals as may be specified by him and any expenditure incurred in connection with such audit shall be payable by the State Commission to the Comptroller and Auditor-General.

(3) The Comptroller and Auditor-General or any person appointed by him in connection with the audit of the accounts of the State Commission under this Act shall have the same rights and privileges and the authority in connection with such audit as the Comptroller and Auditor-General generally has in connection with the audit of Government accounts and, in particular, shall have the right to demand the production of books, accounts, connected vouchers and other documents and papers and to inspect any of the offices of the State Commission.

(4) The accounts of the State Commission, as certified by the Comptroller and Auditor-General or any other person appointed by him in this behalf, together with the audit report thereon, shall be forwarded annually to the State Government by the State Commission and the State Government shall cause the audit report to be laid, as soon as may be after it is received, before the State Legislature.

CHAPTER VIII

MISCELLANEOUS

36. Matters not subject to jurisdiction of the Commission

(1) The Commission shall not inquire into any matter which is pending before a State Commission or any other Commission duly constituted under any law for the time being in force.

(2) The Commission or the State Commission shall not inquire into any matter after the expiry of one year from the date on which the act constituting violation of human rights is alleged to have been committed.

37. Constitution of special investigation teams

Notwithstanding anything contained in any other law for the time being in force, where the Government considers it necessary so to do, it may constitute one or more special investigation teams, consisting of such police officers as it thinks necessary for purposes of investigation and prosecution of offences arising out of violations of human rights.

38. Protection of action taken in good faith

No suit or other legal proceeding shall lie against the Central Government, State Government, Commission, the State Commission or any Member thereof or any person acting under the direction either of the Central Government, State Government, Commission or the State Commission in respect of anything which is in good faith done or intended to be done in pursuance of this Act or of any rules or any order made thereunder or in respect of the publication by or under the authority of the Central Government, State Government, Commission or the State Commission of any report paper or proceedings.

39. Members and officers to be public servants

Every Member of the Commission, State Commission and every officer appointed or authorised by the Commission or the State Commission to exercise functions under this Act shall be deemed to be a public servant within the meaning of section 21 of the Indian Penal Code.

40. Power of Central Government to make rules

(1) The Central Government may, by notification, make rules to carry out the provisions of this Act.

(2) In particular and without prejudice to the generality of the foregoing power, such rules may provide for all or any of the following matters namely:-

(a) the salaries and allowances and other terms and conditions of service of the [Chairperson and Members][1] under section 8;

(b) the conditions subject to which other administrative, technical and scientific staff may be appointed by the Commission and the salaries and allowances of officers and other staff under sub-section (3) of section 11;

(c) any other power of a civil court required to be prescribed under clause (f) of sub-section (1) of section 13;

(d) the form in which the annual statement of accounts is to be prepared by the Commission under sub-section (1) of section 34; and

(e) any other matter which has to be, or may be, prescribed.

(3) Every rule made under this Act shall be laid, as soon as may be after it is made, before each House of Parliament, while it is in session, for a total period of thirty days which may be comprised in one session or in two or more successive sessions, and if, before the expiry of the session immediately following the session or the successive sessions aforesaid, both Houses agree in making any modification in the rule or both Houses agree that the rule should not be made, the rule shall thereafter have effect only in such modified form or be of no effect, as the case may be; so however, that any such modification or annulment shall be without prejudice to the validity of anything previously done under that rule.

40A. Power to make rules retrospectively—The power to make rules under clause (b) of sub-section (2) of section 40 shall include the power to make such rules or any of them retrospectively from a date not earlier than the date on which this Act received the assent of the President, but no such retrospective effect shall be given to any such rule so as to prejudicially affect the interests of any person to whom such rule may be applicable.

Power of Commission to make Regulations[1]

[2][**40(B)** (1) Subject to the provisions of this Act and the rules madethereunder, the Commission may, with the previous approval of the Central Government, by notification, make regulations to carry out the provisions of this Act.

(2) In particular and without prejudice to the generality of the foregoing power, such regulations may provide for all or any of the following matters, namely:-

(a) the procedure to be followed by the Commission under sub-section(2) of Section 10;

(b) the returns and statistics to be furnished by the State Commission;

(c) any other matter which has to be, or may be, specified by regulations.

(3) Every regulation made by the Commission under this Act shall be laid, as soon as may be after it is made, before each House of Parliament, while it is in session, for a total period of thirty days which may be comprised in one session or in two or more successive sessions, and if, before the expiry of the session or the successive sessions aforesaid, both Houses agree in making any modification in the regulations or both Houses agree that the regulation should not be made, the regulation shall thereafter have effect only in such modified form or be of no effect, as the case may be; so however, that any such modification or annulment shall be without prejudice to the validity of anything previously done under that regulation.]

41. Power of State Government to make rules

(1) The State Government may, by notification, make rules to carry out the provisions of this Act.

(2) In particular and without prejudice to the generality of the foregoing power, such rules may provide for all or any of the following matters, namely :

(a) the salaries and allowances and other terms and conditions of service of the Chairperson and Members under section 26;

(b) the conditions subject to which other administrative, technical and scientific staff may be appointed by the State Commission and the salaries and allowances of officers and other staff under sub-section (3) of section 27;

(c) the form in which the annual statement of accounts is to be prepared under sub-section (1) of section 35.

(3) Every rule made by the State Government under this section shall be laid, as soon as may be after it is made, before each House of the State Legislature where it consists of two Houses, or where such Legislature consists of one House, before that House.

42. Power to remove difficulties

(1) If any difficulty arises in giving effect to the provisions of this Act, the Central Government, may by order published in the Official Gazette, make such provisions, not inconsistent with the provisions of this Act as appear to it to be necessary or expedient for removing the difficulty.

Provided that no such order shall be made after the expiry of the period of two years from the date of commencement of this Act.

(2) Every order made under this section shall, as soon as may be after it is made, be laid before each House of Parliament.

43. Repeal and Savings

(1) The Protection of Human Rights Ordinance, 1993 is hereby repealed.

(2) Notwithstanding such repeal, anything done or any action taken under the said Ordinance, shall be deemed to have been done or taken under the corresponding provisions of this Act.

Appendix-III

FUNDAMENTAL RIGHTS

Part III of Indian Constitution (Article 12-35)

Articles

12. Definition - In this Part, unless the context otherwise requires, "the State" Includes the Government and Parliament of India and the Government and the Legislature of each of the States and all local or other authorities within the territory of India or under the control of the Government of India.

13. **Laws inconsistent with or in derogation of the fundamental rights-**

1. All laws in force in the territory of India immediately before the commencement of this Constitution, in so far as they are inconsistent with the provisions of this Part, shall, to the extent of such inconsistency, be void.
2. The State shall not make any law, which takes away or abridges the rights conferred by this Part and any law made in contravention of this clause shall, to the extent of the contravention, be void.
3. In this article, unless the context otherwise requires, -
   (a) "law" Includes any Ordinance, order, byelaw, rule, regulation, notification, custom or usage having in the territory of India the force of law;
   (b) "laws in force" includes laws passed or made by a Legislature or other competent authority in the territory of India before the commencement of this Constitution and not previously repealed Right to Equality
4. Nothing in this article shall apply to any amendment of this constitution made under Article 368. (inserted by the constitution 24th Amendment Act, 1971, Section 12)

14. **Equality before law** - The State shall not deny to any person equality before the law or the equal protection of the laws within the territory of India.

15. **Prohibition of discrimination on grounds of religion, race, caste, sex or place of birth -**

1. The State shall not discriminate against any citizen on grounds only of religion, race, caste, sex, and place of birth or any of them.
2. No citizen shall, on grounds only of religion, race, caste, sex, place of birth or any of them, be subject to any disability, liability, restriction or condition with regard to-
   (a) access to shops, public restaurants, hotels and places of public entertainment; or

(b) the use of wells, tanks, bathing *ghats*, roads and places of public resort maintained wholly or partly out of State funds or dedicated to the use of general public.

3. Nothing in this article shall prevent the State from making any special provision for women and children.
4. Nothing in this article or in clause (2) of Article 29 shall prevent the State from making any special provision for the advancement of any socially and educationally backward classes of citizens or for the Scheduled Castes and the Scheduled Tribes.
5. Nothing in this article or in sub-clause (g) of clause (1) of article 19 shall prevent the State from making any special provision, by law, for the advancement of any socially and educationally backward classes of citizens or for the Scheduled Castes or Scheduled Tribes in so far as such special provisions relate to their admission to educational institutions including private educational institutions, whether aided or unaided by the State, other than the minority educational institutes referred to in clause (1) of article 30.

16. **Equality of opportunity in matters of public employment-**

1. There shall be equality of opportunity for all citizens in matters relating to employment or appointment to any office under the State.
2. No citizen shall, on grounds only of religion, race, Caste, sex, descent, place of birth, residence or any of them, be ineligible for, or discriminated against in respect of, any employment or office under the State.
3. Nothing in this article shall prevent Parliament from making any law prescribing, in regard to a class or classes of employment or appointment to an office under the Government of, or any local or other authority within, a State or Union territory, any requirement as to residence within that State or Union Territory prior to such employment or appointment.
4. Nothing in this article shall prevent the State from making any provision for the reservation of appointments or posts

in favour of any backward class of citizens which, in the opinion of the State, is not adequately represented in the services under the State.

4A. Nothing in this article shall prevent the State from making any provision for reservation [in matters of promotion, with consequential seniority, to any class] or classes of posts in the services under the State infavour of the scheduled Castes and Scheduled Tribes which, in the opinion of the State, are not adequately represented in the services under the State.]

4B. Nothing in this article shall prevent the State from considering any unfilled vacancies of a year which are reserved for being filled up in that year in accordance with any provision for reservation make under clause (4) or clause (4a) as a separate class of vacancies to be filled up in any succeeding year or years and such class of vacancies shall not be considered together with the vacancies of the year in which they are being filled up for determining the ceiling of fifty percent reservation to total number of vacancies of that year.]

5. Nothing in this article shall affect the operation of any law which provides that the incumbent of an office in connection with the affairs of any religious or denominational institution or any member of the governing body thereof shall be a person professing a particular religion or belonging to a particular denomination.

17. **Abolition of Untouchability** - "Untouchability" is abolished and its practice in any form is forbidden. The enforcement of any disability arising out of "Untouchability" shall be an offence punishable in-accordance with law.

18. **Abolition of titles** -

1. No title, not being a military or academic distinction, shall be conferred by the State.
2. No citizen of India shall accept any title from any foreign State.
3. No person who Is not a citizen of India shall, while he holds any office of profit or trust under the State, accept without the consent of the President any title from any foreign State.

4. No person holding any office of profit or trust under the State shall, without the consent of the President, accept any present, emolument, or office of any kind from or under any foreign State.

19. **Right to Freedom**

Protection of certain rights regarding freedom of speech, etc. -

1. All citizens shall have the right -
   (a) to freedom of speech and expression;
   (b) to assemble peaceably and without arms;
   (c) to form associations or unions;
   (d) to move freely throughout the territory of India;
   (f) to reside and settle in any part of the territory of India; and
   (g) to practice any profession, or to carry on any occupation, trade or business.

2. Nothing in sub-clause (a) of clause (1) shall affect the operation of any existing law, or prevent the State from making any law, in so far as such law imposes reasonable restrictions on the exercise of the right conferred by the said sub-clause in the interests of the sovereignty and integrity of India, the security of the State, friendly relations with foreign States, public order, decency or morality, or in relation to contempt of court, defamation or incitement to an offence.

3. Nothing in sub-clause (b) of the said clause shall affect the operation of any existing law in so far as it imposes, or prevent the State from making any law imposing, in the Interest of the sovereignty and Integrity of India or public order, reasonable restrictions on the exercise of the right conferred by the said sub-clause.

4. Nothing in sub-clause (c) of the said clause shall affect the operation of any existing law in so far as it imposes, or prevent the State from making any law imposing, in the Interests of the sovereignty and Integrity of India or public order or morality, reasonable restrictions on the exercise of the right conferred by the said sub-clause.

5. Nothing in sub-clause (d) and (e) of the said clause shall affect the operation of any existing law in so far as it Imposes, or prevent the State from making any law imposing, reasonable restrictions on the exercise of any of the rights conferred by the said sub-clauses either in the interests of the general public or for the protection of the interests of any Scheduled Tribe.

6. Nothing In sub-clause (g) of the said clause shall affect the operation of any existing law in so far as it Imposes or prevent the State from making any law Imposing, in the Interests of the general public, reasonable restrictions on the exercise of the right conferred by the said sub-clause, and, in particular, nothing in the said sub-clause shall affect the operation of any existing law in so far as It relates to, or prevent the State from making any law relating to,-

(i) the professional or technical qualifications necessary for practising any profession or carrying on any occupation, trade or business, or

(ii) the carrying on by the State, or by a corporation owned or controlled by the State, of any trade, business, industry or service, whether to the exclusion, complete or partial, of citizens or otherwise.

20. **Protection in respect of conviction for offences:**

1. No person shall be convicted of any offence except for violation of a law in force at the time of the commission of the act charged as an offence, nor be subjected to a penalty greater than that which might have been Inflicted under the law in force at the time of the commission of the offence.

2. No person shall be prosecuted and punished for the same offence more than once.

3. No person accused of any offence shall be compelled to be a witness against himself.

21. **Protection of life and personal liberty:-** No person shall be deprived of his life or personal liberty except according to procedure established by law.

21A. **Right to Education:-** The state shall provide free and compulsory education to all children of the age of six to fourteen years in such manner as the state may, by law determine. (Inserted by Constitution (86th Amendment) Act, 2002 date 12-12-2002)

22. **Protection against arrest and detention in certain cases -**

1. No person who is arrested shall be detained in custody without being informed, as soon as may be, of the grounds for such arrest nor shall he be denied the right to consult, and to be defended by, a legal practitioner of his choice.

2. Every person who is arrested and detained in custody shall be produced before the nearest magistrate within a period of twenty-four hours of such arrest excluding the time necessary for the journey from the place of arrest to court of the magistrate and no such person shall be detained in custody beyond the said period without the authority of a magistrate.

3. Nothing in clauses (1) and (2) shall apply

(a) to any person who for the time being is an enemy alien; or

(b) to any person who is arrested or detained under any law providing for preventive detention.

4. No law providing for preventive detention shall authorise the detention of a person for a longer period than three months unless-

(a) an Advisory Board consisting of persons who are, or have been, or are qualified to be appointed as, Judges of a High Court has reported before the expiration of the said period of three months that there is in its opinion sufficient cause for such detention :

Provided that nothing in this sub-clause shall authorise the detention of any person beyond the maximum period prescribed by any law made by Parliament under sub-clause (b) of clause (7)

(b) or such person is detained in accordance with the provisions of any law made by Parliament under sub-clauses (a) and (b) of clause (7).

5. When any person is detained in pursuance of an order-made under any law providing for preventive detention, the authority making the order shall, as soon as may be communicate to such person the grounds on which the order has been made and shall afford him the earliest opportunity of making a representation against the order.

6. Nothing in clause (5) shall require the authority making any such order as is referred to in that clause to disclose facts which such authority considers to be against the public interest to disclose.

7. Parliament may by law prescribe

(a) the circumstances under which, and the class or classes of cases in which, a person may be detained for a period longer than three months under any law providing for preventive detention without obtaining the opinion of an Advisory Board in accordance with the provisions of sub-clause (a) of clause (4);

(b) the maximum period for which any person may in any class or classes of cases be detained under any law providing for preventive detention ; and

(c) the procedure to be followed by an Advisory Board in an Inquiry under sub-clause (a) of clause (4).

23 Right against Exploitation

Prohibition of traffic in human beings and forced labour -

1. Traffic in human beings and *begar* and other similar forms of forced labour are prohibited and any contravention of this provision shall be an offence punishable in accordance with law.

2. Nothing in this article shall prevent the State from imposing compulsory service for public purposes, and In imposing such service the State shall not make any discrimination on grounds only of religion, race, caste or class or any of them.

24. Prohibition of employment of children in factories, etc. - No child below the age of fourteen years shall be employed to work in any factory or mine or engaged in any other hazardous employment.

25 Right to Freedom of Religion

Freedom of conscience and free profession, practice and propagation of religion -

1. Subject to public order, morality and health and to the other provisions of this Part, all persons are equally entitled to freedom of conscience and the right freely to profess, practise and propagate religion.

2. Nothing in this article shall affect the operation of any existing law or prevent the State from making any law -

(a) regulating or restricting any economic, financial, political or other secular activity, which may be associated with religious practice;

(b) providing for social welfare and reform or the throwing open of Hindu religious Institutions of a public character to all classes and sections of Hindus.

Explanation 1 - The wearing and carrying of *kirpans* shall be deemed to be included in the profession of the Sikh religion.

Explanation II- In sub-clause (2), the reference to Hindus shall be construed as including a reference to persons professing the Sikh, Jaina or Buddhist religion, and the reference to Hindu religious institutions shall be construed accordingly.

26. **Freedom to manage religious affairs** - Subject to public order, morality and health, every religious denomination or any section thereof shall have the right-

(a) to establish and maintain institutions for religious and charitable purpose;

(b to manage its own affairs in matters of religion;

(c) to own and acquire movable and immovable property; and

(d) to administer such property in accordance with law.-

27. **Freedom as to payment of taxes** for promotion of any particular religion - No person shall be compelled to pay any taxes, the proceeds of which are specifically appropriated in payment of

expenses for the promotion or maintenance of any particular religion or religious denomination.

28. **Freedom as to attendance at religious** instruction or religious worship in certain educational institutions -

1. No religious instruction shall be provided in any educational institution wholly maintained out of State funds.

2. Nothing in clause (1) shall apply to an educational institution which is administered by the State but has been established under any endowment or trust which requires that religious instruction shall be imparted in such Institution.

3. No person attending any educational institution recognised by the State or receiving aid out of State funds shall be required to take part in any religious instruction that may be imparted in such Institution or to attend any religious worship that may be conducted in such institution or in any premises attached thereto unless such person or, if such person is a minor, his guardian has given his consent thereto.

29 Cultural and Educational Rights

Protection of interests of minorities -

1. Any section of the citizens residing in the territory of India or any part thereof having a distinct language, script or culture of its own shall have the right to conserve the same.

2. No citizen shall be denied admission into any educational Institution maintained by the State or receiving aid out of State funds on grounds only of religion, race, caste, language or any of them.

30 **Right of minorities to establish and administer educational Institutions -**

1. All minorities, whether based on religion or language shall have the right to establish and administer educational institutions of their choice.

lA. In making any law providing for the compulsory acquisition of any property of an educational institution established and administered by a minority, referred to in clause (1), the State shall ensure that the amount fixed by or determined under such law for the acquisition of such property is such as would not restrict or abrogate the right guaranteed under that clause.

2. The State shall not, in granting aid to educational Institutions, discriminate against any educational Institution on the ground that it is under the management of a minority, whether based on religion or language.

31C. **Saving of laws giving effect to certain directive principles-**

Notwithstanding anything contained in Article 13, no law giving effect to the policy of the State towards securing all or any of the principles laid down in Part IV shall be deemed to be void on the ground that it is inconsistent with or takes away or abridges any of the rights conferred by Article 14 or Article 19; and no law containing a declaration that it is for giving effect to such policy shall be called in question in any court on the ground that it does not give effect to such policy....

32 Right to Constitutional Remedies

Remedies for enforcement of rights conferred by this Part-

1. The right to move the Supreme Court by appropriate proceedings for the enforcement of the rights conferred by this Part is guaranteed.

2. The Supreme Court shall have power to issue directions or orders or writs, including writs in the nature of *habeas corpus*, *mandamus*, prohibition, *quo- warranto* and *certiorari,* whichever may be appropriate, for the enforcement of any of the rights conferred by this part.

3. Without prejudice to the powers conferred on the Supreme Court by clauses (1) and (2), Parliament may by law empower any other court to exercise within the local limits of its jurisdiction all or any of the powers exercisable by the Supreme Court under clause (2).

4. The right guaranteed by this article shall not be suspended except as otherwise provided for by this Constitution.

33. **Power of Parliament to modify the rights conferred by this Part in their application to Forces, etc. -**

Parliament may, by law, determine to what extent any of the rights conferred by this Part shall/ in their application to,-

(a) the members of the Armed Forces; or

(b) the members of the Forces charged with the maintenance of public order; or

(c) persons employed in any bureau or other organisation established by the State for purposes of intelligence or counter intelligence; or

(d) persons employed in, or in connection with, the telecommunication systems set up for the purposes of any Force, bureau or organisation referred to in clauses (a) to (c), be restricted or abrogated so as to ensure the proper discharge of their duties and the maintenance of discipline among them.

34. **Restriction on rights conferred by this Part while martial law is in force in any area** - Notwithstanding anything in the foregoing provisions of this Part, Parliament may by law indemnify any person in the service of the Union or of a State or any other person in respect of any act done by him in connection with the maintenance or restoration of order in any area within the territory of India where martial law was in force or validate any sentence passed, punishment inflicted, forfeiture ordered or other act done under martial law in such area.

Part IV

DIRECTIVE PRINCIPLES OF STATE POLICY

36. **Definition** - In this Part, unless the context otherwise requires, "the State" has the same meaning as in Part III.

37. **Application of the principles contained in this Part** - The provisions contained in this Part shall not be enforceable by any court, but the principles therein laid down are nevertheless fundamental in the governance of the country and it shall be the duty of the State to apply these principles in making laws.

38. **State to secure a social order for the promotion of welfare of the people** –

1. The State shall strive to promote the welfare of the people by securing and protecting as effectively as it may a social order in which justice, social, economic and political, shall inform all the Institutions of the national life.

2. The State shall, in particular, strive to minimize the inequalities in income, and endeavour to eliminate inequalities In status, facilities and opportunities, not only amongst individuals but also amongst groups of people residing in different areas or engaged in different vocations.

39. **Certain principles of policy to be followed by the State-** The State shall, in particular, direct its policy towards securing -

(a) that the citizen, men and women equally, have the right to an adequate means of livelihood;

(b) that the ownership and control of the material resources of the community are so distributed as best to subserve the common good;

(c) that the operation of the economic system does not result in the concentration of wealth and means of production to the common detriment;

(d) that there is equal pay for equal work for both men and women;

(e) that the health and strength of workers, men and women, and the tender age of children are not abused and that citizens are not forced by economic necessity to enter avocations unsuited to their age or strength;

(f) that children are given opportunities and facilities to develop in a healthy manner and in conditions of freedom and dignity and that childhood and youth are protected against exploitation and against moral and material abandonment.

39A. **Equal justice and free legal aid** - The State shall secure that the operation of the legal system promotes justice, on a basis of equal opportunity, and shall, in particular, provide free legal aid, by suitable legislation or schemes or in any other way, to ensure that opportunities for securing justice are not denied to any citizen by reason of economic or other disabilities.

40. Organisation of village *panchayats* - The State shall take steps to organise village *panchayats* and endow them with such powers and authority as may be necessary to enable them to function as units of self-government.

41. **Right to work, to education and to public assistance in certain cases** - The State shall, within the limits of its economic capacity and development, make effective provision for securing the right to work, to education and to public assistance in cases of unemployment, old age, sickness and disablement, and in other cases of undeserved want.

42. **Provision for just and humane conditions of work and maternity relief-**

The State shall make provision for securing just and humane conditions of work and for maternity relief.

43. **Living wage, etc., for workers** - The State shall endeavour to secure, by suitable legislation or economic organisation or in any other way, to all workers agricultural, industrial or otherwise, work, a living wage, conditions of work ensuring a decent standard of life and full enjoyment of leisure and social and cultural opportunities and, in particular, the State shall endeavour to promote cottage industries on an individual or cooperative basis in rural areas.

43 A. **Participation of workers in management of industries-** The State shall take steps, by suitable legislation or in any other way, to secure the participation of workers in the management of undertakings, establishments or other organisation engaged in any industry.

44. **Uniform civil code for the citizens** -The State shall endeavour to secure for the citizens a uniform civil code throughout the territory of India.

45. **Provision for free and compulsory education for children-** The State shall endeavour to provide, within a period of ten years from the commencement of this Constitution, for free and

compulsory education for all children until they complete the age of fourteen years.

46. **Promotion of educational and economic interests of Scheduled Castes, Schedule Tribes and other weaker sections**- The State shall promote with special care the educational and economic interests of the weaker sections of the people, and in particular, of the Scheduled Castes and the Scheduled Tribes, and shall protect them from social injustice and all forms of exploitation.

47. **Duty of the State to raise the level of nutrition and the standard of living and to improve public health** - The State shall regard the raising of the level of nutrition and the standard of living of Its people and the improvement of public health as among its primary duties and, in particular, the State shall endeavour to bring about prohibition of the consumption except for medicinal purposes of intoxicating drinks and of drugs which are injurious to health.

48. **Organisation of agriculture and animal husbandry-**

The State shall endeavour to organise agriculture and animal husbandry on modern and scientific lines and shall, in particular, take steps for preserving and improving the breeds, and prohibiting the slaughter, of cows and calves and other *milch* and draught cattle.

48 A. **Protection and improvement of environment and safeguarding of forests and wild life**- The State shall endeavour to protect and improve the environment and to safeguard the forests and wild life of the country.

49. **Protection of monuments and places and objects of national importance** –

It shall be the obligation of the State to protect every monument or place or object of artistic or historic interest, declared by or under law made by Parliament to be of national importance, from spoilation, disfigurement, destruction, removal, disposal or export, as the case may be.

50. **Separation of Judiciary from executive** -

The State shall take steps to separate the judiciary from the executive in the Public Services of the State.

51. **Promotion of international peace and security-**

The State shall endeavour to –

(a) promote international peace and security;

(b) maintain just and honourable relations between nations;

(c) foster respect for international law and treaty obligations in the dealings of organised people with one another; and

(d) encourage settlement of international disputes by arbitration.

Appendix -IV

National Commission for Minorities

National Minorities Commission was formed in January 1978 through a Government Resolution, which stated, "Despite the safeguards provided in the Constitution and the Laws in force, there persists among the Minorities a feeling of inequality and discrimination. In order to preserve secular traditions and to promote National Integration the Government of India attaches the highest importance to the enforcement of the safeguards provided for the minorities and is of the firm view that effecting institutional arrangements are urgently required for the enforcement and implementation of all safeguards provided for the minorities in the Constitution, in the Central and State laws and in Government policies and administrative schemes enunciated from time to time. The Government of India has therefore, resolved to set up a Minorities Commission to safeguard the interest of the Minorities whether based on religion or language."

At Center the Minority Commission was set up in 1978 where as in Uttar Pradesh it was set up in 1960 with ten members (one chairman and nine members). In the meanwhile Bihar set up a multi-member Minority Commission in 1971. Subsequently Gujarat also set up the commission for minorities.

The Central Minorities Commission consisted of a Chairman and two other members for three years. A Parsi and two members from Christian and Muslim headed the first Minorities Commission. The appointment of Parsi was greatly resented by the Muslim who constituted the biggest minority in the country. Therefore, the Commission was reconstituted on July 28, 1978. While a Muslim was appointed as its Chairman its four members were taken from the Buddhist, Christian, Parsi and Sikh Communities.

The Janata Government of Morarji Desai wanted to confer the constitutional status on the Central Minorities Commission. It introduced the 46th Constitutional Amendment Act, 1978 in Lok Sabha which to abolish the office of Special Officer for Linguistic Minorities provided for in Article 350-B and to add Article 338-A to make room for a constitutional sanctioned Minorities Commission. The amendment said "The Government are of the view that appointment of a commission to safeguard the interest of all minorities, whether based on religion or language, would provide a more satisfactory institutional arrangement for achieving the desired objective. A Minorities Commission was, therefore, set up by an executive order. Such a Commission would, if set up in pursuance of Constitutional provision, inspire greater confidence among the Minorities." In 1979, the bill was again introduced in the Lok Sabha as 51st Amendment Bill, but the bill again fell due to lack of necessary support.

In 1984 the Commission was detached from the Home Ministry and placed under the Ministry of Welfare. The Commission suffered another setback in 1987 when it was robbed of its jurisdiction over the Linguistic Minorities of the country. Thus, the commission was reduced to the position of a helpless caretaker for Religious Minorities only. The non-implementation of the provision of 1978 Resolution that the Special Officer for Linguistic Minorities would act as the Secretary of the Commission also rendered the Commission less effective. In 1988 the Congress Government constituted a new Commission. It firmly turned down the suggestion that the commission should be given either constitutional or ordinary legislative status, or conferred powers exercisable under the Commissions of Inquiry Act, 1952.

After the overthrow of the Congress Government and emergence of a non-Congress government under V. P. Singh, a fresh demand was raised for according constitutional status to the commission. However, V. P. Singh government could not make necessary constitutional amendment in this regard, because the government had been formed with the support of BJP, which was not willing to permit him to equate the status of Minorities Commission with the Scheduled Castes Commission.

The Congress modified its stand on the Minorities Commission after the assassination of Rajiv Gandhi and promised to accord it constitutional status. But when it came to power in 1991 it decided to accord statutory status to the commission instead of constitutional status. In May 1992, Sitaram Keshari, the Welfare Minister introduced National Commission for Minorities Bill in the Lok Sabha. Justifying the Bill he said, "The Minorities Commission with a statutory status would infuse confidence among the Minorities about the working and effectiveness of the Commission. It would also carry more weight with the State Government/ Union Territory/Administrations and the ministries/ departments and other organisations of the Central Government." But the bill was strongly opposed by L. K. Adwani, the leader of opposition in the House. He described the bill as 'ill-conceived and retrograde'. He even admitted that he felt guilty of having been a party to the creation of Minorities Commission in 1978. Despite this opposition the Lok Sabha eventually passed the Bill. Subsequently it was passed by Rajya Sabha and the President gave his assent on May 17,1992.

National Commission for Minorities Act, 1992

The National Commission for Minorities Act, 1992 provided for a seven-member Commission. The Government from amongst persons of eminence, ability and integrity appoints the Chairman and the other members of the Commission. Five members of the Commission, including the Chairman are taken from the Minority communities. The procedure for selection of the chairman and members of the commission has been left to the discretion of the Government. The Chairman and other members of the Commission hold office for a term of three years. They can resign earlier by addressing the Central Government. The Chairman and member can also be removed from office if he (i) becomes an undischared insolvent; (ii) is convicted and sentenced to imprisonment for an offence which, in the opinion of the Central Government, involves moral turpitude; (iii) becomes unsound mind and declared so by the competent court; (iv) refuses to act or becomes incapable of acting; (v) absents himself from three consecutive meetings of the Commission without leave or absence; (vi) has in the opinion of the Central Government abused his position and his continuance in office is detrimental to the interests of the minorities or public interests. When a person is to be removed he must be given a reasonable opportunity of being heard in the matter.

For the smooth working of the Commission the Central Government provides a secretary and such other officers and employees as are necessary for efficient performance of the function of the Commission. These employees and officers are given such salaries and allowances, which are prescribed from time to time. The salaries and allowances of the Chairmen, members and administrative staff are paid out of grant provided by the Central Government.

The composition of the National Minorities Commission was modified in September 1995 through an amendment in the Act. A new post of Vice-Chairman was created, even though he still continued to be counter as a member.

In May 1992 the National Commission for Minorities Act, 1992 was enacted giving statutory status to the erstwhile Minorities Commission and thus making it a more effective body to safeguard the interest of Minorities.

The functions of the commission have been stipulated in Article 9 (10) of the Act are:

1. To evaluate the progress of the development of minorities under the Union and States;
2. To monitor the working of the safeguards provided in the Constitution and in laws enacted by Parliament and State Legislatures;
3. To make recommendation for effective implementation of the safeguards for the protection of the interests of the minorities by the Central Government or State Governments;
4 To look into specific complaints regarding deprivation of rights and safeguards of the minorities and take these up with appropriate authorities;
5. To undertake studies into problems arising out of discrimination against minorities and recommend measures for their removal;
6. To conduct studies, research and analysis on issues relating to socio-economic and educational development of minorities;

7. To suggest appropriate measures in respect of any minority to be undertaken by the Central Government or the State Governments;
8. To make periodical or special reports to the Central Government on any matter pertaining to the minorities and in particular difficulties confronted by them;
9. To consider any other matter which may be referred to it by the Central Government.

The Commission submits an annual report to the government, which is tabled by the government before each House of Parliament along with a memorandum explaining the action taken or proposed to be taken on the recommendations relating to the Union and the reasons for non-compliance, if any, of such recommendations.

Index

E

F

G

H

N

O

P

T

U